BOOKS BY RALPH S. CUSHMAN

I HAVE A STEWARDSHIP
PRACTICING THE PRESENCE
SPIRITUAL HILLTOPS
DEAR BOB

I HAVE A STEWARDSHIP

A Book of Worship

RALPH S. CUSHMAN

A BISHOP OF THE METHODIST CHURCH

ABINGDON-COKESBURY PRESS

NEW YORK • NASHVILLE

CUSHMAN
I HAVE A STEWARDSHIP

Copyright, 1939, by
Ralph S. Cushman

Printed in the United States of America

TO MY MOTHER

NELLIE HONEY CUSHMAN

February 3, 1857—August 3, 1938

GOOD NIGHT, MOTHER MINE

Life is so wonderful, life such as thine;
Death cannot end it, dear mother of mine!
Morning will come again gilding the trees,
Spring notes will sound again sweet on the breeze!

This is not dying, my brave mother dear,
Thou art but climbing up out of The Here,
Out of thy struggles and out of thy pain,
Out where with Christ life will flower again.

So, then, good night, mother, only good night;
Turn thy dear face to the mansions of light.
Life is so wonderful, life such as thine;
Death cannot end it! Good night, mother mine!

Contents

A Foreword

"Why stand ye gazing up into heaven?" (Acts 1. 11.)

THE best way—perhaps the only way—to save worship from becoming mere heaven-gazing is to link it up with stewardship. There is something to do! I have a stewardship entrusted to me!

On the other hand, I believe that the most effective way to teach the New Testament principles of Christian stewardship is to put them into the form of devotional studies. Worship and stewardship must cleave together. The way of stewardship is a sure way to God. "Not every one that saith unto me, Lord, Lord, shall enter into the kingdom of heaven; but he that doeth the will of my Father" (Matthew 7. 21).

The churches of America deeply need a revival of Christian Stewardship, if for no other reason than to awaken millions of inactive members. It is not merely that the Kingdom progress is being blocked by these indifferent ones, but their own souls are certainly in peril of becoming dwarfed. Moreover, the moral life of our nation is at stake, for as goes the Church so goes the State!

I am happy to acknowledge the helpful criticism which these studies have received from my wife, Maud Hammond Cushman. I am likewise grateful for the untiring service which my secretary, Lottie B. Spyker, has given to the preparation of this manuscript.

These messages are largely the product of my own morning-watch hour, and I send them forth with the

hope and prayer that others may catch the vision that
has been given me in the Upper Room.

> Stir me awake, dear God,
> New days are calling;
> Stir me awake, awake,
> New days are here!

R. S. C.

CHAPTER ONE

𝕴 𝕳𝖆𝖛𝖊 𝖆 𝕾𝖙𝖊𝖜𝖆𝖗𝖉𝖘𝖍𝖎𝖕

I

A DISCIPLE'S DISCOVERY

"I have a stewardship entrusted unto me" (1 Corinthians 9. 17, A. R. V.).

SAINT PAUL is speaking. "I have a stewardship," he cries. "Whether I like it or don't like it; whether I get a reward or don't get a reward; I face the fact; I have a stewardship!"

"I have a stewardship." Read between the lines and hear what Paul has many times said to himself. "I have a stewardship. I can't get away from this ever-present truth. In my waking hours it presses on me; when I am asleep it stirs me in my dreams. I have something to do. I have something to be. It is my task and no one else can do my work. If I don't do it, it will not be done. God help me, I have a stewardship!

"It is God-given, this stewardship. Some day I will have to answer to my Maker. I can never get away from Him. I have tried; I know! 'Whither shall I . . . flee from Thy presence? . . . If I take the wings of the morning, and dwell in the uttermost parts of the sea; even there shall thy hand lead me and thy right hand shall hold me' (Psalm 139. 7-10).

"But how strange that I should ever have tried to get away from God! That is what it meant, to flee from this stewardship of mine. Blessed was the day

11

when I learned the truth, when I made the discovery, that to take up my stewardship was to find God and life. O life that is everlasting! Yes, and with it joy and peace and power. Oh, it was to find myself! Thanks be to God, I have a stewardship!"

Paul was a great adventurer—a great spiritual discoverer! God bless to us his memory lest we forget. That is the trouble with us, we forget. We forget that, whether we like it or not, we have a stewardship; every one of us has a stewardship! There is no inactive membership in the Kingdom of Christ, even if sometimes we seem to think there is in the Church on earth.

But, someone says, to be a Christian is to believe. Yes, it is, but to believe so deeply that we must do something about it. Too much of our believing isn't believing at all. Does a man really believe a truth until that truth moves him to action?

It is indeed a great truth that Adventurer Paul is disclosing to the Corinthians. Would that we all might grasp it! He says, "Necessity is laid upon me; for woe is unto me, if I preach not the gospel" (1 Corinthians 9. 16, A. R. V.). The Christian is a compelled person. When he accepts Christ, he is given a stewardship. It is in the form of a cross. It is his whether he accepts it or not. And woe unto him if he accepts it not!

But we must not be misled by the word "preach." Paul is not putting professional preachers in one group and professing Christians in another. The preaching that Paul is talking about is witnessing—witnessing to what God has done for us through Jesus Christ. Did not Jesus command this of *all* disciples? He said, "Ye shall be my witnesses . . . unto the uttermost part of the earth" (Acts 1. 8). Truly, every Christian is

called to say, "I have a stewardship." But do we really
understand what Saint Paul is saying in this scripture?
*"For if I preach the gospel, I have nothing to glory of;
for necessity is laid upon me. . . . For if I do this of
mine own will, I have a reward: but if not of mine
own will, I have a stewardship entrusted to me"* (1
Corinthians 9. 16-17, A. R. V.).

* * *

A Prayer

O God, for Christ's sake, who loved us and gave
Himself for us, help us this day to see life as a trust
from Heaven, an opportunity to bring the eternal life
from above down to earth. And if in hours of weakness the battle seems too hard and we grow faint, help
us still to stand! Remind us then that to the faithful
is the road to power and peace and God. Amen.

Meditation

"God has a life plan for every human life in the
eternal counsels of His will. When He arranged the
destiny of every star and every sand-grain and every
grass blade and each of those tiny insects which live
but for an hour, the Creator had a thought for you
and me. It was a thought of what we were to be, of
what we might become, of what He would have us to
do with our days and years of influence with our
lives."—*Henry Drummond*.

This Day

This day, Lord, is Thy gift of grace,
Wherein I may discern Thy face!
The sunbeams quivering on a tree
Reveal Thy constant care for me;
This glad green earth, the blue above,
May tell the wonders of Thy love.

But oh, dear Lord, lest blind my eyes
Should grow to all Thy wide-lifting skies,
To all Thy gifts of earth and sea,
Lord, keep Thy loving hand on me;
Lest as I journey on my way
I miss the glories of each day!

II

HANGED UP HARPS

"It is required in stewards, that a man be found faithful"
(1 Corinthians 4. 2, A. R. V.).

So Saint Paul insists, "I have a stewardship!"
Whether I face life's responsibilities willingly or unwillingly, the unavoidable fact confronts me: life is a
God-given trust. If I accept this trust willingly, trust-
ingly, so much the better for me. I get a reward. How
rich are God's rewards! But if unwillingly I face life,
if I stand halting before the challenges of this present
hour, my unwillingness does not change the eternal
truth that life is a stewardship just the same.

Indeed, Paul would say, "Whether you are a Christian or a Jew or a pagan—whatever you are—every
created child of God has a stewardship to answer for."
"To whomsoever much is given, of him shall much be
required" (Luke 12. 48, A. R. V.). Everyone entrusted
with life will have to answer for that trust. Indeed,
God's universe is created on that basis. Once upon a
time there was a soured philosopher who cried, "I
accept the universe." And there was a wiser man who
replied, "Well, you'd better!"

"Oh, the little more, and how much it is!
And the little less, and what worlds away!"

"It is required of a steward that a man be found
faithful," regardless of time and place or how he feels

or the circumstances that surround him. His own welfare is at stake on his faithfulness. How ridiculous the
stewards of God can make themselves sometimes in
the face of difficulties! This is the picture of the 137th
psalm. One of the temptations we all need to pray
to be delivered from is the surrender to self-pity! It
is too enervating; it is blighting.

Yet that is exactly what the captive Israelites in this
psalm are doing. "By the waters of Babylon there
we sat down. We wept. We hanged up our harps!"
Now, harps were not made to be hanged up. They
were made to be played where music is most needed.
But they whined, "How can we sing the Lord's song
in a strange land?"

No, we don't have to be unsympathetic toward these
distressed people who had been dragged away from
Jerusalem. But it is easy to see that they were hurting
themselves more than their captors by refusing to sing
when they needed song most. And yet we of today
must be careful in our criticism, for we may have
heard of professing Christians in some of our own
churches who have had their feelings hurt over trifling
things, and they have hanged up their harps. So
Christ suffers again and again, and the Kingdom
movement is stalled, because we forget that it is
required of a steward that a man be found faithful,"
regardless of his feelings!

So for the Christian it is a thousand times evident
that life is a trust that tests us. As Maltby Babcock
put it,

> "We are not here to play, to dream, to drift;
> We have hard work to do and loads to lift;
> Shun not the struggle: face it—'tis God's gift."

Face it, for it is God's gift! And now at this very

point we must understand Paul's message. He is really asking the question: How do we face life? With its long procession of struggles and hardships, of victories and defeats, how do I face the burdens and responsibilities of the years, willingly or reluctantly? Paul declares that whichever way I accept these things, it does not change the fact that life is a stewardship just the same. "For," he says, "if I do this thing of mine own will, I have a reward" (1 Corinthians 9. 17, A. R. V.). What kind of a reward? When and where? We must look into that!

But suppose I face life unwillingly, selfishly, what then? Well, it will be just too bad for *me*. Angels will weep over me. Christ will try to plead with me. But it will not change the everlasting truth of God's universe. "It is required in stewards that a man be found faithful." It is required!

* * *

A Prayer

"O Lord God, give me the desire to be persistent in service while I have the health and strength. May I experience the sweetness that comes in doing the thing that I ought to have done as well as that in which I took most pleasure. Help me so to live that my days may be Thy days, through Jesus Christ, my Lord. Amen."—*Margaret Bird Steinmetz*.

Meditation

"Thank God every morning when you get up that you have something to do that day which must be done, whether you like it or not. Being forced to work and forced to do your best will breed in you temperance, self-control, diligence, strength of will, content, and a hundred virtues which the idle will never know."—*Charles Kingsley*.

Undefeated

Out of the shame of my coward heart,
   Out of my night of defeat,
Lift me, O God, to the battle again,
   Cover my bitter retreat!

Out of despising my weakness and rout,
   Out of the love of Thy soul,
Purge me, oh, purge, with Thy hyssop, dear Christ,
   Give me my spirit made whole!

Beaten, but still undefeated, I pray,
   Thou of unconquerable hand,
Reach me my poor broken saber again,
   I pledge Thee to die or to stand!

By the wonders of Heaven's forgiveness,
   By the lovely lure of Thy light,
By the spirit of victory eternal,
   God fling me again to the fight!

III

THE SINGING HEART

"My heart is fixed, O God;
  I will sing, . . .
  Awake, psaltery and harp" (Psalm 108. 1, 2, A. R. V.).

"I *will* sing! Awake, psaltery and harp." That sounds interesting, especially after reading about people who hanged up their harps and whined over their troubles. "I will sing!" That sounds like the story of a man who could sing but didn't feel like singing; yet who knew that he ought to sing and needed to sing; and then after a fight with himself cried, "I will!" "My heart is fixed—I *will* sing!" That is what the consciousness of a God-given stewardship can do for a person.

Indeed, this is exactly the story of Missionary Dan Crawford, of African fame. In his *Journal* he tells how a wave of homesickness swept over him as he became swallowed up in the jungle. Then it grew fearfully dark. What a long time would have to pass before he would see again the dear shores of the home land! He thought of the obstacles ahead. Perhaps his adventure was unwise. Then he lost his song. The days passed—days of increasing gloom. He couldn't sing. And then one morning—blessed be holy habits!—he read the 108th psalm (R. V.):

> "My heart is fixed, O God;
> I will sing"—

"I will!"—and sing he did until the jungle was transformed into a heavenly place, and the darkness sped away.

I think in Dan Crawford's story we have the key to what Saint Paul means when he speaks of the reward for willing stewardship. "If I do this thing willingly, I have a reward" (1 Corinthians 9. 17). If I sing, whether I feel like it or don't feel like it, pretty soon I begin to feel like it! And "the feeling like it" is just then our great reward.

So the rewards of life—we must see—are not to be thought of as in the next world alone. They are here in this world. Every day we can see them. Of course they are in the next world too, but there are a lot of people who might be saved from retribution in the next world, and whose lives would be far happier in this, if they would quit presuming on the mercy of God both for the next world and for the here and now. "Whatsoever a man soweth, that shall he also reap."

There is judgment in the background of these lovely lines which Mrs. Browning gave the world:

> "Thy love shall chant its own beatitudes
> After its own life working. A child's kiss
> Set on thy sighing lips shall make thee glad;
> A poor man served by thee shall make thee rich;
> A sick man helped by thee shall make thee strong;
> Thou shalt be served thyself by every sense
> Of service which thou renderest."

But the meaning is deeper than the poet's lines might suggest. The ultimate reward of willing stewardship is the abounding life which God gives through companionship with Himself in Christ. And the New Testament makes it clear that the growth of this fellowship with Christ depends finally upon the fixed heart and the faithful stewardship. I may have an experience of God in some Aldersgate Street or on some Mount of Transfiguration, but if I am to keep this experience and have it grow, I must learn how to walk with God in daily faithfulness.

Yes, and let us say it again: I must learn to be faithful when I feel like it and when I don't! And sooner or later we reach that happy day when too we always feel like it. Blessed reward!

* * *

A Prayer

Blessed Christ, Thou hast taught us that through Thee we may have life and have it more abundantly. We beseech Thee to purify our vision, that being enabled to see Thee as the enlarger of all life, we may perfectly abandon ourselves to Thy holy will and find in Thee our largest consummation and joy. Amen.

Meditation

"On the night of Saturday, May 29th, he [Dan Crawford] accidentally injured the hand, and although it was carefully dressed by Mrs. Crawford, the trouble became more serious. At 2 P. M. on Wednesday, June 2, 1926, the mail having arrived, he dictated his last communications. Said he: "My left arm is poisoned, and this poison is knifing my very heart; so we are in God's hands and all is well. It is harrowing and might have been avoided. . . . Good-by, dear friends; we will meet at the appearing in excellent glory.' "—*British Weekly*.

Dan Crawford's Passing

"My left arm is burning; this poison
    Is knifing deep down in my heart!"
So he wrote, that great soul of the jungle,
    So he wrote, then made ready to start!

Brave soldier of Christ, naught could daunt him!
    Had he quailed before Africa's night?
New adventure! That's all; God is calling!
    "Good-by, friends, we will meet in the light!"

"All's well!" Crawford said it, we feel it!
    In God's hands, good warrior, lie down.
Yes, we'll meet you "in excellent glory,"
    But we'll miss you the wide world around!

IV

THE STRAITENED WAY

"Narrow is the way which leadeth unto life" (Matthew 7. 14).

Think of it, a narrow way leading unto life! I have never liked narrow things. My college days bred that in me. It was twenty-five years before I could preach on this scripture, "Narrow is the way which leadeth unto life."

Then it came to me that the same Jesus who said, "I am come that they might have life," also said, "Enter ye in at the strait gate." Evidently, there must be some real connection between finding life—the blessed God life—and walking the narrow way. Indeed, that is just what Jesus says here, "Narrow is the way which leadeth unto *life*."

There is food for thought here; Jesus points out two roads. These roads lead across the years. Let us study them. The first road is a broad way; it has no strait gates. Indeed, there are no fences. There are the wide open spaces! Plenty of room to go where you please. There are no signs, "Keep off" from anything, or "Watch your step!" It sounds good! And yet Jesus warns, Beware! this road "leadeth to destruction."

The other road has a narrow gate and fences too; and who hasn't itched to get over fences? And there are signs up: "Danger!" "Watch your step!" True, off there in the distance are the beckoning mountains, snow-capped and adventurous-looking. But who likes narrow gates and straitened ways? Yet Jesus says this way leads to life—glorious life! What does all this mean?

I know two young couples who got married. It was a straitened way for both. But the one pair wouldn't see it. The fact that the salary was small was no reason why these two shouldn't have everything their friends were having. They must entertain; they must dress as well. But each month they spent a little more than they earned. And each month when the bills came in, lo, the lovers quarreled! And yet they shied away from the narrow gate and the only way that might have saved them. At length the crash came. The parents refused to help out longer. The creditors did the same. Then the divorce! Jesus said, "Broad is the way that leadeth to destruction."

The other couple chose the straitened way from the start. It was not easy, but it was their only hope of being good stewards of a great love. They too had friends who "had things." They too were tempted to follow the crowd; but they clung to the road! They spent a little less than they earned. They invested in insurance against the future. Sometimes Jane shed a few tears when sacrifices seemed too great. But still they clung to the road.

So the years passed and one morning as a family of five sat at a comfortable breakfast table, and as Jim read a few verses from Matthew's Gospel about a "strait gate" and a "narrow" way the children heard their mother say, "Jim, I guess we have known something about that straitened way." And the answer came, "Yes, dear, and we know too where the road leads. Life is wonderful!"

Did you ever climb a mountain peak? Well, it is a thrilling business. But it takes all there is in you, including a clear mind and a strong heart; and from the start it is a straitened way and a rough road. And generally the nearer the top the narrower grows the way. But look at the view! Breathe the air! Just so, Jesus said, "Narrow is the way which leadeth unto life!"

* * *

A Prayer

"Search me, O God, and know my heart: try me,

and know my thoughts; and see if there be any wicked way in me, and lead me in the way everlasting." And this I ask in Jesus' name. Amen.

Meditation

"Nothing earthly will cause me to give up my work in despair. I encourage myself in the Lord God, and go forward."—*David Livingstone.*

"Man, by living wholly in submission to the Divine Influence, becomes surrounded with, and creates for himself, internal pleasures infinitely greater than any he can otherwise attain to—a state of heavenly Beatitude."—*J. P. Greaves.*

The Heights

It seems to me the fairest flowers these eyes have seen,
  With fullest fragrance and in colors rare,
Are those which drink the sweetness of the mountain peaks,
  And flourish in the sunshine of the mountain air!

And can it be, my soul, that life grows strong,
  That beauty deeper and more fragrant crowns our day,
As we, with tired feet but hearts undaunted still,
  Push upward, ever upward, on our way?

What matter if the heights be hard to gain,
  What matter if the road must narrow be,
With every turn the fairer vision grows;
  Lord, let me walk the mountain peaks with Thee!

V

None of Our Business

"Is it nothing to you, all ye that pass by?" (Lamentations 1. 12.)

"It isn't any of our business, is it, Lord?" Only a little child, whose conscience had not been hardened, could pray a prayer like that.

She had seen a poor man on the street that day, in evident need. "Oh, mama," she had said, "let's help him!"

The mother's answer was, "Come along, dear, it isn't any of our business."

But that night, after she had said her "Now I lay me down to sleep," she added, "O God, bless that poor man on the corner." And then remembering her mother's words, "But really, it isn't any of our business is it, Lord?" The tragic fact is that too many of us grow up in that pagan philosophy that the world about us is none of our business—unless, indeed, the needs and heartbreaks of the world come too near.

But the Voice that troubled the little girl at prayer has troubled complacent souls in all generations. It was the same Voice that said, "Is it nothing to you, all ye that pass by?"

Jerusalem is in ruins! The prophet of God, looking down on broken walls and a ruined Temple, is deeply stirred. It seems like the end of the world to him. But off there in the distance caravans are passing: commerce is going north and south; business as usual! How terrible this indifference! But to the prophet this city is still a living thing—fallen, wounded, wrecked. And to the sensitive soul of the man of God comes a pleading cry—the cry of the City of God, "Is it nothing to you, all ye that pass by?"

But that sentence could be applied to every generation. God is forever trying to build His city. A congressional investigation committee is telling us just now that Communism is a real menace to America. Too bad that we could not have realized the peril to

Russia two generations ago, when a certain Christian statesman was appealing to the American churches to put a million dollars into the evangelizing of that country. And what of China? I shall not forget the missionary who yesterday sat before me and exclaimed: "It's a shame! Think of it, American Christians collecting scrap iron and selling it to Japan to help her soldiers murder my Christian converts!" Oh, is it nothing to you, all ye that pass by?

Yes, think of our America. How save our country from being pagan? For instance, think of the ten millions and more of American children who are receiving no religious education in any church or synagogue. Is it any of our business?

Think of the ruin that the revived liquor traffic is making in our country. Homes ruined, youth started on the wrong road. And some churchmen still drinking the peril and others even selling it. Oh, is it nothing to you, ye church people?

Why is it that we have so many so-called "inactive members" in all the churches? One sure reason is that we have never taught them to say with Saint Paul as they face the moral and spiritual needs of every community, "I have a stewardship!"

A good steward is one who never says, "It is none of our business." Every problem in the world is the business of every Christian in the world. Didn't Jesus tell us to pray, "Thy kingdom come on earth"? And didn't He say too, "He that hath my commandments, and keepeth them" (underscore those two words, "keepeth them"), "he it is that loveth me: . . . and I will love him, and will manifest myself unto him"? (John 14. 21.) Then how can we expect to have fellowship with Christ unless we seek with Him the sharing life?

It must have been a man who said there are two kinds of women in the world, "Those who take the strength out of you and those who put it back." At any rate, there are two kinds of people in the world. Those who share and those who don't. Hear Jesus, "Inasmuch as ye did it unto one of these my brethren, *even* these least, ye did it unto me" (Matthew 25. 40, A. R. V.).

* * *

A Prayer

O Thou Compassionate One, strengthen us again to meet the day's demands; the calls are so many, the needs so vast, and we are so weak; we pray to Thee again for strength. Forgive our selfishness and our sins. For the sake of Thy kingdom and the Cause, gird us anew. In Jesus' name. Amen.

Meditation

"In a beautiful Southern garden, amidst lovely roses, I saw a young woman and a little child. The sky was clear and blue, but the child did not know; the birds sang, but she did not hear. In a wild rage she threw herself upon the soft grass and kicked and screamed. The young woman's face was full of compassion as she stooped to lift the child; tears filled her eyes as she thought of the long years before that little soul, imprisoned by bars stronger than steel. Suddenly the teacher's face grew strong and tender. She would break the bars; and in that great moment she took

upon herself all the handicaps of the little child!"—
Margaret Slattery (on Helen Keller's teacher).[1]

The Glorious Minority

There are people who carry life's burdens,
  Their own and some others beside;
There are people who stand in their places,
  And who stand there whatever betide.

When the Kingdom is calling for workers,
  Or the city is crying for men,
Or some cause is seeking supporters,
  These people will answer just then.

You may know where to find them in darkness,
  You may know where to find them by day:
And when your load presses down hardest,
  You will find they are going your way.

There are two kinds of people—you know them
  As you journey along on life's track—
The people who take your strength from you,
  And others who put it all back.

VI

STOLEN THUNDER

"None of us liveth to himself" (Romans 14. 7).

"Do you believe that a country can get along without religion?"

The question was a surprise because the questioner had been unconsciously irritating me for a half hour with his perpetual profanity.

We were in Moscow, Russia. Just as our group had started to go through a cotton mill we were joined by four New England millowners also on a tour of

---

[1] *He Took It Upon Himself.* The Fleming H. Revell Company.

inspection. It was my lot to pair off with one of these men. I don't suppose he knew how blasphemous was his ordinary conversation. Some men don't. I had endured it about as long as I could when he burst out with the question, "Do you believe that a country can get along without religion?" I suppose that New Englander was trying to point out the menace of a godless government. When I got my breath I replied to the profane religionist—and I hope he got the point—"Well, it makes a big difference what you mean by religion." So it does! It wouldn't hurt any of us to examine our own definition! A modern American writer has said that our churches are full of people to whom religion is hardly more than an "inherited bit of propriety!"

But the Russian Bolshevists took religion more seriously. They said, "Religion is an opiate." And so they have been trying to destroy it. What they mean is that religion is a sort of "escape mechanism" by which men seek to flee from the challenges of this world into the contentment of the next. "What has the Church ever done for the workers?" they shout.

Of course it is the cry of ignorance, and too of rank and godless materialism. But, nevertheless, isn't the downfall of the Russian Church a warning to us all? Do we know the sharing life? Do we not have in most of our churches too many members in whose souls the vision of the better world arouses little enthusiasm? Oh, how we need a revival of Christian stewardship—a new breed of members who understand Paul's cry, "I have a stewardship"!

I can yet see that young Russian. He had come to our hotel in Moscow. He had come to tell us of the youth organization to which he and hundreds of thousands of young men and women belonged. In order to join one had to declare war against "religion" and the idea of "God." He surprised us by his emphasis upon the ideals of his organization. He spoke enthusiastically of their educational campaign against some moral problems. Then he proceeded to tell us about his life as a worker. Seven hours a day he labored. "But," he said, "some of us belong to the shock troops, and our hours are longer."

"What are the shock troops?" we asked.

He replied: "We give the government one, two, three, or more hours a day after our work. We are thrown in where the Five-Year Plan is dragging. It's a contribution we make!" he said with spirit.

Someone replied, "Well, at that rate you don't get much time for recreation, do you?" I shall never forget the light that flashed into the young man's eyes as he faced us almost fiercely, and answered: "No, we of the shock troops don't get much time for recreation now." "But," he added, "you must remember that here in Russia we are building the better world!"

Now, where did these Russians learn this talk about building a new world? To me it is perfectly clear. They have stolen the Christian's thunder! While Karl Marx, and Lenin, and the rest of them repudiate and attack religion, nevertheless they have taken from the Gospels the vision of a new world as Jesus proclaimed it.

Stolen thunder! It surely is. This "better-world" challenge was the dominant note of our Lord Jesus. "When ye pray," Jesus commanded, "say, Thy kingdom come, . . . on earth as it is in heaven."

Why has the Church failed so long to emphasize those two key words, "on earth"? I rather believe that one of the reasons is that so many professing Christians have not yet found Christ's definition of religion. And this is what was behind Saint Paul's words, "None of us liveth to himself." And you just can't live unto yourself and live! Everyone who tries to comes to the same end. Life goes stale on him, becomes blasted, dies! Real life is a stewardship.

* * *

A Prayer

O Lord Jesus, who for our redemption didst come to earth, cleanse our hearts, we pray, from all selfish ambition; and grant us so to be stirred by Thy passion for the world, that faithfully following Thee, we may rejoice in Thy final victory, to the glory of Thy holy name. Amen.

Meditation

"Jesus taught us to make every human interest we touch as precious as our own, and to treat all persons with whom we deal as members of that beneficent system of mutual good will which is the Kingdom of Heaven."—*William DeWitt Hyde.*

Set Us Afire

Set us afire, Lord,
  Stir us, we pray!
While the world perishes
  We go our way,
Purposeless, passionless,
  Day after day.
Set us afire, Lord,
  Stir us, we pray!

VII

CHRIST'S AMBASSADORS

"We are ambassadors therefore on behalf of Christ" (2 Corinthians 5. 20).

It is told of E. Stanley Jones that in India a railroad-train attendant objected to his entering a certain compartment, saying, "There is a diplomat within." But when the missionary with a smile replied, "Oh, but I am the ambassador of a King," the attendant stepped aside.

Why not? If we could only realize the honor of the commission conferred upon us by Christ, what new power it would give us among the sons of earth! Saint Paul says, "If any man is in Christ, *he is* a new creature." Of course he is! He is a changed man. He has been born into the royal family. How petty are the pomp and glory of the world compared with this!

But it is no mere empty honor that has been conferred upon us. It is an ambassadorship; and it means work to be done, for it cost a great price. What price? Nothing less than God's gift of His Son! No wonder that Paul exclaims, "The love of Christ constraineth us"! Constraineth us how? Why, to look upon our ambassador's commission as a mighty honor and a joyous responsibility. For Christ "died for all, that they that live should no longer live unto themselves but unto him who for their sakes died, and" (don't forget those last words!) "rose again"! Our King is unconquerable!

But do we appreciate this honor? What is the meaning of these figures before me? They do not come from my own communion, although they do not differ much. Another large denomination has issued this graph: "Seventy-one per cent of the total members do no service in the local church, . . . "

And this from another graph: "Fifty-four per cent of church members give nothing; forty per cent subscribe to the church support by individual and family groups; twenty-seven per cent of total members give all moneys received for world missions; seventy-three per cent give nothing." And we are ambassadors?

I see a picture. We were in Russia just outside the summer place of the Czars. From this place the last Czarina was arrested with her children and started on the sad journey to Siberia and death. More than a score of us—all Americans—had been through the extensive and extravagant rooms of the palace; and now, hot and wearied, we sat down under the shade of the trees in the gardens near the lovely lake. We were not alone; there were scores of Russian workmen on their rest day, enjoying the freedom of the park.

"Why not talk with some of these workmen?" Finally two young men were brought in who consented to answer our questions.

That was one of the most interesting hours of that summer. Indeed, two hours would be more exact. The crowd began to gather. Very soon there were about two hundred Russian workmen, men and women, not only listening to our questions, but replying with questions of their own—questions about conditions in America. Sometimes they were embarrassing!

Finally we asked one of the young men a question that seemed to stir the crowd. I shall never forget his answer. It was the apparently harmless question, "Do you belong to The Party?" Now, in the membership of the Communist Party at that time there were about two million souls, but these two million were so well organized and disciplined that they held in an iron grip the remaining one hundred and sixty million people in that vast country.

The young man heard our question with something of surprise and apparent glee. "Oh, no," he said, "I don't belong to The Party. Not yet! You know it's a great honor and a big responsibility to belong to The Party. You have to be tested first. Some day—after I have proved myself—I hope to belong to The Party."

Immediately there came into my mind the thought of our church membership back in America. I lay back on the grass and, closing my eyes, I murmured, "O God, help our people at home to feel the honor and responsibility of membership in the Church of Christ as truly as these Russian workmen feel the honor of membership in The Party."

* * *

A Prayer

Dear Christ, may we live so near Thee this day as to be conscious of Thy passion to remake the world, and of the infinite resources at Thy command. For Thine is the kingdom and the power and the glory forever. Amen.

Meditation

"Christianity has not been tried and found wanting; it has been found difficult and not tried."—*G. K. Chesterton.*

The Vision Splendid

This is our vision splendid!
    This is our world's one hope
Amid earth's devastation
    For us who dare the slope,
For us who dream in darkness,
    For us who dream of light,
Who hold the faith eternal
    That wrong shall yield to right,

That nations build a brotherhood,
    That strife and wars shall cease,
That color lines shall vanish
    Amidst a reign of peace,
That greed and human heartlessness
    Shall finally give way
Before the angels' singing
    And the Kingdom's glad new day!

This is our vision splendid
    When doubts and fears assail,
And hopes and dreams long battled for,
    Are trembling in the gale;
Behold our vision splendid
    Transfiguring the cross,
Transforming death to victory
    And making gain of loss!

Dear Christ, our vision splendid,
    One glimpse into Thy face,
One grasp upon Thy mighty hand,
    Shall stir the world apace;
O Son of Man from Heaven,
    O Lord of love and grace,
Behold our devastation,
    Rebuild this human race!

CHAPTER TWO

Jesus' Philosophy of Life

I

MY FATHER'S BUSINESS

"I must be about my Father's business" (Luke 2. 49).

WE began with Saint Paul. Exerything in his life seemed to say, "I have a stewardship!"

But where did he get this vision and this passion? The foundation must have been laid in the faith of his fathers. How great a gift it is to be well born! How loyally we should guard our nobler inherited characteristics!

But a new birth came to Saul of Tarsus that afterday when he met the living Christ on the Damascus road. Life was never the same after that.

> "The touch of a hand, the flash of an eye,
> A glimpse of the face of a passer-by,
> A challenging word on a busy street,
> And afterward life is incomplete!"

So it was on that Damascus road. Saint Paul never got away from the face of Christ calling to him there. And, strangely enough, in the center of the vision was a cross!

"God forbid," cries Paul, "that I should glory, save in the cross of our Lord Jesus Christ" (Galatians 6. 14). It must be that the apostle found joy in the cross. It sounds like it. Anyway, in that cross and in that Christ the valiant Saul of Tarsus found a new philosophy of life.

We shall see that there is a vital relation between Saint Paul's slogan, "I have a stewardship," and Jesus' words in today's scripture. Since the beginning of human existence men and women have been searching for a satisfactory philosophy of life. And forget not that the search begins in the very young.

A few years ago, in a city of New York state where I was a pastor, a young college boy put a bullet through his head and left behind to his cultured but pagan parents this note of explanation. He said, "I can't see that life is worth the living." It turned out that he belonged to a little college group that had labeled itself, "The Society of the Godless"! Indeed, unless there is a good God with a good purpose behind the universe, life must be a terrible puzzle. At times one might easily say with the pagan poet:

"Yet Ah, that Spring should vanish with the rose!
That Youth's sweet-scented manuscript should close!
    The nightingale that in the branches sang,
Ah, whence, and whither flown again, who knows!"

Who knows? There are many who do; as did Saint Paul, following Jesus. In his book, *The Five Great Philosophies of Life,* William DeWitt Hyde points out the various attempts of man to frame a constructive purpose of life. There was the Epicurian who maintained that "pursuit of pleasure is the real end of life." There was the Stoic who preached "self-control by law." There was the Platonist who advocated a mystic but selfish asceticism. And there were the disciples of the great Aristotle who propounded a somewhat lofty gospel—but for the few!

But the philosophy of Jesus was not for the few. On that first Christmas night the angels sang of "good tidings of great joy, which shall be to *all* people."

Evidently, the outstanding difference between Jesus' conception of what life is for and the pagan conception lies in three words that Jesus uses, "My Father's business." How wonderful to feel that the God behind the universe is "My Father"! Then to have a conviction that there is "a purpose behind it all"!

Rather strange, is it not, that even as good a mother as Mary should have failed to realize that a twelve-year-old boy is not too young to begin to frame a philosophy of life? "And he said unto them, How is it that ye sought me? wist ye not that I must be about my Father's business?" (Luke 2. 46-49.)

* * *

A Prayer

"O Lord of Hosts, who has given us our station and our weapons in thine army for the warfare of this life, setting comrades beside us and sending Jesus Christ before us; make us to feel the glory and strength of thy victorious advance and to hear triumph song where Christ marches at the head of his saints, conquering, and to conquer; for his sake. Amen."—*The Indian Prayer Cycle.*

Meditation

"I know that you have a philosophy, each and all of you, and that the most interesting and important thing about you is the way in which it determines the perspective in your several worlds. . . . The philosophy which is so important in each of us is not a technical matter; it is our more or less dumb sense of what life honestly and deeply means."—*William James.*

Gift of Gifts

Life is worth while, dear God,
To those who know
This rich companionship with Thee;
Each morning as the day flames forth,
Each evening in a sweet tranquillity.

Ten million million gifts
Spring from Thy hand,
Of up-flung mountains, evening skies, a tree!
Yet never one can quite compare with this—
The giving of Thyself to me!

II

Dreams of Youth

"The Spirit of the Lord is upon me" (Luke 4. 18).

Home is the most interesting place in the world.
Perhaps because there we see people just as they are,
with all the restraints thrown off—too much so some
times! But, anyway, we come to know one another,
the good things about us, and the bad.

In today's scripture Jesus comes home! To Nazareth,
"where he was brought up." What a flood of mem-
ories must have come over Him! So it is with all of
us when we go back home. But no one really knows
very much about Jesus' boyhood. Yet that fact hasn't
prevented poets and others from drawing pictures of
Him. One of the boyhood happenings that Jesus
must have recalled when He came home was that Pass-
over season when, with the caravan of neighbors, He
went up to Jerusalem and "got lost." Or was it His
mother and father who got lost?

Mary has been criticized for not keeping more careful watch on her boy. How could a mother let three
days go by without knowing just where He was?

Well, perhaps, after all, she was a wiser parent than some of us.

But I wish I might have seen her face when that twelve-year-old boy in the Temple looked straight into His mother's eyes and said with all the earnestness that youth can muster, "How is it that ye sought me? wist ye not that I must be about my Father's business?"

I wonder if Mary at that moment didn't recall that she had seen that same look in His face at other times —perhaps after He had spent a day alone in the mountains above Nazareth. I wonder if Mary at such times didn't lift her heart in prayer to Heaven in some such words as a modern poet has pictured:

> "I know, Lord, Thou hast sent him—
>
> . . . .
>
> But Thou hast only lent him—
> His heart's for Thee!
>
> "But e'en when he was nursing,
> A baby at my breast,
> It seemed he was dispersing
> The world's unrest."[1]

"Dispersing the world's unrest"—a magnificent phrase! And who can conceive of a nobler task? And this was the vision and passion of the boy Jesus when He said, "I must be about my Father's business." That was a great dream to get into a boy's soul.

What American youth needs today is some challenging "Cause." Something he can call, "My Father's business." Recently someone declared that modern youth is the finest the world has ever known—more intelligent, more highly cultured, better appearing than the youth of any previous generation; *but that*

---

[1] Cale Young Rice. Used by permission.

he lacks the one thing that sets a youth afire and makes him outstanding, namely, "some great cause."

"While the youth in the Orient is marching, and the youth in Germany is marching, and youth in Russia is marching, and youth in Italy is marching, it is not so in America." In spite of statements to the contrary, youth in America is having too much done for him, they say. He himself is not being stabbed into new life and purpose and by some great Cause. Well, it is worth thinking about. Probably we would never have known the name of Saul of Tarsus had he not cried, "I have a stewardship!"

Today, as Jesus comes back home to Nazareth, the old sense of "my Father's business" is still upon Him— only more so! Can we understand His feelings that Sabbath morning in the old home church, when He read that Old Testament dream and ended by saying, "This day is this scripture fulfilled in your ears"?

"The Spirit of the Lord is upon me, because he hath anointed me to preach the gospel to the poor; he hath sent me to heal the broken-hearted, to preach deliverance to the captives, and recovering of sight to the blind, to set at liberty them that are bruised, to preach the acceptable year of the Lord" (Luke 4. 18, 19).

* * *

A Prayer

O Shepherd of Israel, Thou that leadest Thy people like a flock, lead us this day! The tasks are so great, and we are so small. The burdens are so heavy, and we are so weak. Let Thy Heavenly Spirit sustain us with Thy power, that, having borne the burdens of the day, we may be led into Thy rest by Jesus Christ our Lord. Amen.

Meditation

"God is a kind Father. He sets us all in the place where He wishes us to be employed; and that employment is truly 'our Father's business.' "—*John Ruskin.*

Life Is So Strange

Life is so strange!
I lay awake last night.
You ask me why?
And I can't tell—exactly,
Only I have lost my boy!

And you won't understand
Unless you too have lost a pal,
A boy, who walked with you the fields,
And jumped with you the brooks,
Together with you climbed the trees.

You watched him as he grew,
You told him all the secrets of the skies
And of your hopes for him.
And, then, one day, you came to realize
That you'd lost your boy!

Yes, life is strange!
I lay awake last night!
How did I lose him?
That's the rub; I lost him
Just as my old Dad lost me.

There came a girl!
And I need say no more.
But just the same
I lay awake last night;
I know I've lost my boy.

Yes, I have lost my pal,
And now I walk the fields alone;
Alone I walk the woods beside the brook,
And everywhere I see old footprints—
Marks of him—but he has gone!

I think that in the great Beyond
That there must be a place
Where Dads find once again their pals.
And yet I can't exactly understand
How such a thing could be.
Life is so strange!

III

A NEW EARTH

"Thy kingdom come. Thy will be done in earth" (Matthew 6. 10).

What was the difference between the word of the boy Jesus to His mother in the Temple and His message to His neighbors in the old home church at Nazareth? Really, there was very little difference. The stewardship passion was the same. And the dream—the God-given dream—was the same. Only it had matured; twenty years had passed. In the Temple it was "my Father's business." But at Nazareth Jesus told them some of the details of the dream: good news for the poor, healing for broken-hearted, deliverance for captives, sight for blind, liberty to the bruised!

What a new world that will be when the dreams of Jesus come to pass and the Kingdom shall come on earth! Some of the hymn writers have dreamed over again this dream of Jesus, and we have learned to sing,

"The Kingdom is coming, O tell ye the story,
  God's banner exalted shall be!
The earth shall be full of His knowledge and glory,
  As waters that cover the sea."

But we have sung too thoughtlessly and carelessly! We haven't taken Jesus' dream of a New World too seriously. At least we haven't done too much about it.

When I was a boy in college in New England, I went over to a neighboring city to hear the man who was one of the greatest preachers in the United States at that time, Dr. George A. Gordon, of Boston. It was a college congregation, and he began his message by telling of "an old professor over at Amherst who always began every semester in the same way."

He would begin: "There is one thing that I ought to say at the very start. To you who think you can skin through this course in the same way that you try to skin through all the other courses in this college: I just want to say to you that it can't be done. You will get out of this course exactly what you put into it. And, if you put nothing in, that is exactly what you will get out."

Doctor Gordon drew himself up to his full height and said: "Our churches are full of people like that. They seem to think they can skin through their religious duties here on earth, and then at last skin into heaven. I want to tell you young people that it cannot be done!" It is about thirty years since that Boston preacher spoke those words, but I have not forgotten how he went on to say, "The trouble with most of these church members is that *they have never understood what the call of Christ really is.*"

Is it true that millions of our members have never understood? Have never understood "what the call of Christ really is"? Only today I heard a Christian educator say a similar thing as he discussed the challenge of America to the Church. He said, "I find myself embarrassed by the fact that there are some sixty million church members in America, and yet America is more than one half pagan." Then he added, "How can we Christianize this pagan half of the State until we have Christianized the pagan half of the Church?"

Can Doctor Gordon's statement be true? Have we

any considerable number of church members who do not really know what it is all about, save that the religion of Christ is somehow an escape mechanism against trouble in the world to come?

Thanks be to God, I can still hear, across thirty years, a layman speaking: "It is a great thing to be a Christian. If there were no Hereafter, it would be worth it all to have Christ transforming our lives and our homes right now in this world."

Well, that is exactly what He came to do! Not to get us into heaven but to get heaven into us for all time and eternity. Who can read Jesus' message at Nazareth without realizing that it was a redeemed world of redeemed persons He was seeking?

O that we might feel the passion that He put into that prayer, "Thy kingdom come, thy will be done on earth as it is in heaven!"

* * *

A Prayer

Blessed Holy Spirit, who hast promised to make intercession for us in our hours of need, hear us, we beseech Thee, at the beginning of this, another day. So illumine our minds by Thy holy presence, and so purify and strengthen our hearts by Thy mighty power, that all day long, in word and thought and deed, we may be faithful stewards of the Divine Grace, that Thy kingdom may come, to the glory of Jesus Christ, our Lord. Amen.

Meditation

"It was through the amazing tragedy of Calvary and the marvelous transitions of Pentecost that the ageless mystery of the Trinity became radiant with

meaning. Then they that sat in darkness saw a great
light, by which they read that neither with God in the
heavens, nor among men on the earth, is there an
undistributive reserve of life, or love, or power, or
wisdom, or any resources, material or spiritual, that is
to be sacred to the sole use or enjoyment of any holder
or claimant. That is to say, God made love the key-
note of creation, and from the beginning ordained and
exemplified the principle of stewardship as manifesting
its supreme expression."—*Bishop Earl Cranston.*

Resurrection

Ye who fear death,
Behold the buds are bursting;
Ye who fear death,
Hark, hear the robins sing;
Ye who fear death,
Come see the crocus bringing
Eternal Spring!

Ye who fear death,
See how the trees are greening
Risen to life before the April sun;
Ye who fear death,
Give way to joy and gladness,
New Life's begun!

So has it been
Since days first had beginning,
Glad prophecies of resurrection morn;
Weep not before a closed tomb,
In Joseph's garden
Life is reborn!

IV
MEAT AND DRINK

"My meat is to do the will of him that sent me" (John
4. 34).

I know a man who said to his son, when the latter
was considering the ministry as his lifework, "Son,

stay out of it if you can." Then he added, "Oh, I hope you can't!"

Was that good advice? What was behind it? This: It is a sad mistake for anyone to choose the ministry as a lifework unless he is sure that the Heavenly Father is first choosing him. So Jesus declared, "He hath anointed me to preach the gospel to the poor." It surely is a great thing to feel like that—"He hath anointed me!" And to feel sure of it.

But while the call to the ministry from the beginning has been considered an exclusive call, why may we not suppose that every Christian has been called to the ministry of helping God build His Heaven on earth? Certain it is that Jesus' philosophy of life was built upon the conviction that God does have a purpose for each individual man in the world. It must be a sorry thing, especially in the hours of crisis, to feel any doubt concerning the reality of God and the dominating Purpose behind the world. Whether or not Isaac Watts really wrote these lines often credited to him, they certainly state a common and pathetic truth:

> "Most of us creep into the world
>> And know no reason why we're born
>> Save only to consume the corn,
> The flesh, the fish,
> And leave behind an empty dish."

The difference between most of us and Jesus is that He did know why He was born and what His business on earth was. He had something to do; He had been sent!

In today's scripture we have another illustration of His untiring ministry, a story that would make a thrilling film. A tired Traveler sits beside an ancient

well while His Jewish disciples go yonder into a somewhat hostile Samaritan village for food. As He rests
His tired body by the roadside His mind is active, for
this is Jacob's Well.

Here is where history and tradition meet. A hundred pictures and persons rush through His mind.
But not for long! The pictures of the past give way
before the approach of a woman. Her jug is with her.
She has come from the village for water. And now
what would the friendly Jesus do?

All the customs of His day dictated to Him that He
should remain aloof from a woman and a Samaritan.
And His tired body approved! And then He looked
into her face—and into her heart. Hunger and thirst
were written there. And then that strange conversation began.

Talk about a human-interest story! It is here; it will
bear reading over and over. But in the midst of the
conversation the surprised disciples appeared—surprised that Jesus was talking to a woman and a for-
eigner!

When they got their wits together, the best they
could say was, "Master, don't you want something to
eat?"

He answered, "I have meat to eat that you know not
of."

They said, "Who hath brought him meat?" Still
grieved at the woman!

Jesus replied, "My meat is to do the will of him that
sent me, and to finish his work."

Here in this story are indicated two important characteristics of Jesus' philosophy of life. One is that any
adequate philosophy must be concerned with helping
your neighbor. Indeed, more concerned about your

neighbor's welfare than about observing the proprieties or keeping the customs.

And the other truth is that this philosophy brings its own reward. It is meat and drink! That is what Jesus meant, "My meat is to do the will of him that sent me." How He must have prayed that those disciples would understand!

* * *

A Prayer

Dear Living Lord, under the shadow of the cross Thou didst say, "These things have I spoken unto you that my joy may be in you." Help us this day to so follow Thee in loving service to others that we may be conscious of the joy of the Presence. Amen.

Meditation

"Oh, for God's sake, and the sake of poor souls, bestir yourselves, and spare no pains that may conduce to their salvation. What cause have we to mourn before the Lord that we have so long neglected this good work! If we had but engaged in it sooner, how many more might have been brought to Christ!"—*John Wesley*.

Climb Oftener

I never climb my hilltop
But that I find God there,
Nor look up at His sky but that
His voice is in the air!
I know I cannot see His face
Nor touch a fleshly hand,
But God is on my hilltop
And there's glory on the land.

It never fails! No, never!
He is always waiting there
In midnight dark or when the glow
Of morning fills the air;
His Presence waits me on the hill,
A warming Nearness, strong and still.
O soul, climb oftener to be
With Him who lives and waits for thee.

V

SLEEPLESS

"Rising up a great while before day, he went out, and departed into a solitary place, and there prayed" (Mark 1. 35).

"A great while before day"! Why did He get up that morning—and many other mornings—a great while before day? The best answer I know is that He couldn't sleep. The most of us sleep too well, especially when the world is afire!

More than one missionary on furlough has said, "I can't sleep for thinking of them." But Dr. J. H. Jowett, once hearing such a cry, remarked: "But, my brethren, except I spend a day with my Lord, the trend of my life is quite another way. I cannot think about them because I am so inclined to sleep!"

Recently I read a letter from Dr. Robert Brown and Marion Culley, those terribly pressed heroes of Wuhu Hospital, writing of the sufferings of China and of the horrors of war. I passed *one* sleepless night "thinking of them"; but that was all. How easy it is to forget!

If we really knew what was going on in Germany, how the Church is threatened, and Christians persecuted for their faith; if we could really see the menace to the world of the totalitarian state, how many of us would sleep nights? Would there be any one in America who would say, "It is none of our business"?

If we of America really knew would we sleep on? Oh, if that two thirds of our church members who never have made any real contribution to the Kingdom Movement could only glimpse the Jesus of today's story, would they not awake? See Him there on His bed—"a great while before day." He is thinking, thinking, thinking!

Thinking of what? Oh, the world of people, a world of vast and terrible needs! Thinking, rolling, and tossing, until He could endure it no longer. Then, springing from His bed, throwing His clothes hastily about Him, He went out quietly—but eagerly—"into a solitary place."

"And there he prayed!" What did He say in His prayer? I think I know some of the things He said. Under the bright stars as He strode along, I think He had been repeating, "My Father's business!" "My Father's business!" "My Father's business!" And then, as He knelt beside a rough stone as a kneeling form, I think I hear Him say, "Lo, I am come to do Thy will, O God!"

And I think that His prayers ended in triumph. Victory! That is what prayer is for, to give victory. To bring back the sense of the nearness and the power of God—a new confidence that

> "This is my Father's world,
>   O let me ne'er forget
> That though the wrong seems oft so strong,
>   God is the Ruler yet."

A faithful steward is expected to talk over with the Owner of the vineyard the business before them. When we feel a great burden for the Kingdom Business, when the weight of our stewardship is heavy upon us, what we need is to get away into a solitary place and stay there long enough for God's light to break in upon us, and for His victory to possess us. "And this is the victory that overcometh the world, even our faith!"

* * *

A Prayer

Blessed Christ, Thou who didst promise that Thy disciples might remove mountains, increase our faith; and hold us by Thy mighty hand until doubts shall cease, and we believe. Teach us to tarry in Thy presence until conquered by Thy Spirit we too go forth to triumph in Thy holy name. Amen.

Meditation

"I think my soul was never so drawn out in intercession for others as it has been this night; I hardly ever so longed to live to God, and to be altogether devoted to Him; I wanted to wear out my life for Him. . . . I wrestled for the ingathering of souls, for multitudes of poor souls, personally, in many distant places. I was in such an agony, from sun half-an-hour high till near dark, that I was wet all over with sweat; but O, my dear Lord did sweat blood for such poor souls."—*David Brainerd.*

A Summons

How can I sleep, my soul,
   All the world's waking!
How can I sleep, my soul,
   When hearts are breaking?

Stir me, O soul of mine,
   Hear! God is calling.
Sleep never more, my soul,
   While stars are falling.

Look! Fires flame the sky.
  Is Europe dying?
Bombs bursting in the East!
  Is China crying?

O Thou America,
  What is thy reaping,
If, while all hell's astir,
  Thou art still sleeping?

What shall the new day be?
  Hell bound or heaven?
Wake, Land of mine, awake;
  Give of thy leaven!

How can we sleep, O men,
  When hearts are breaking?
Rise, Church of God, arise,
  Are New Days waking?

VI

AND THIS IS LIFE

"And this is life eternal, that they might know thee" (John 17. 3).

How frequently we hear, "Well, it's life!" Something has happened to an acquaintance or a friend and we remark, "Life is like that."

But Jesus taught that these are really shallow observations about things that happen on the surface of life. Jesus is praying—talking with God—just before He goes to Gethsemane and Calvary. Life would be terrible if behind our Gethsemanes we could not have a deep, wonderful communion with the Father. Jesus can pray even under the shadow of the Cross. "This is life, to know Thee, the only true God."

"It is a great thing to be a Christian!" I recently heard one give such testimony. "It means *life*," he added. "A Christian ought to get more out of life than anybody else." True indeed! Saint Paul speaks of "the life which is in Christ." It is a superior life that God offers in Christ.

This is why Jesus says in our scripture, "This is life eternal." Turn those words around and let them read "eternal life." That means a quality of life. The word "eternal" should not signify future life merely. It is life here and now, and life of such *eternal* character that it will prove its superiority in youth and in age.

> I thank thee just for life,
>   The chance to live,
> To be alive! So great thy gift,
>   If thou dost nothing give
> Beside, it is enough. . . .

But we must note that this life is the stewardship life. Jesus doesn't only say, "This is life," to "know thee the only true God," but in the next verse He adds, "I have finished the work which thou gavest me to do" (John 17. 4). It takes action, work, to consummate life.

> "Work!
> Thank God for the might of it,
> The ardor, the urge, the delight of it,
> Work that springs from the heart's desire,
> Setting the brain and the soul on fire."

Yes, there is a joy in work, any kind of work! But there is a superior and mightier joy in linking oneself with God in His work. And that may mean any part of the world's work—even washing dishes or planting corn. The old shoemaker saw this and said, "My work is to do the will of God; I cobble shoes to pay expenses." The point is so clear that all of us may see it.

> "There is no life divided,
>   O Lord of life, from Thee."

Indeed, we must feel this to know the thrill of *the eternal kind of life*. We see this conviction in Jesus from that first day when the twelve-year-old boy said, "Know ye not that I must be about my Father's business?" Years later He said to the religious leaders who thought more of their orthodoxy than of doing God's work, "My Father worketh hitherto, and I work" (John 5. 17). To His questioning disciples He asserted, "I must work the works of him that sent me, while it is day" (John 9. 4).

Later, when the signal came that the end was near, He cried, "Now is my soul troubled; and what shall I say? Father, save me from this hour." Then—in what might have been a moment of wavering—He glimpsed anew His "Father's business" and prayed, "But for this cause came I unto this hour. Father, glorify thy name." And the answer to His prayer we know. (John 12. 27-28.)

No wonder that He went victoriously—even under the shadow of the cross—into the Upper Room where He prayed, "This is life eternal," and then, "I have finished the work thou gavest me to do."

And no wonder that Pilate was troubled at the composed majesty of Him when He answered the question, "Art thou a king?" "Certainly I am a king," was the answer. "This is why I was born, this is why I came into the world."

A Prayer

"O Thou, in whose presence my soul takes delight;
  On whom in affliction I call,
My comfort by day, and my song in the night,
  My hope, my salvation, my all!

"Restore, my dear Saviour, the light of Thy face;
  Thy soul-cheering comfort impart:
And let the sweet tokens of pardoning grace
  Bring joy to my desolate heart." Amen.

Meditation

"But the climax of demonstration of stewardship
appears in God's application of the principle of stewardship in his sovereign relation. Being all-sufficient
unto himself in his infinite attributes, he, nevertheless,
counts it his chief glory to graciously administer the
exhaustive resources of his material empire for the
benefit of his peopled world."—*Bishop Earl Cranston.*

A Hospital Te Deum

O Life, Thou art rich, Thou art full, Thou art free,
Thou art mine, new each morning returning to me!
Though the night has been long, with no star in the sky,
Though its winds those of pain like the sob and the sigh,
Yet, O Life, how I feel, with the first streaks of day,
Thou art mine! To know Thee—this the prayer that I
    pray.

To know Thee, O Life Giver! It is this that I see,
In this glory of living which bursts over me;
To be with Thee and in Thee, Thou life of my life—
What of pain, or of cloud, or of night with its strife!
I am Thine, Thou art mine—Life! abundant and free
And forever! O glad contemplation of Thee!

VII

Joy and Victory

"That my joy might remain in you, and that your joy
might be full" (John 15. 11).

John Ruskin once said, "We may always be sure,
whatever we are doing, that we cannot be pleasing
Him if we are not happy ourselves." Because Jesus

will not tolerate the pagan philosophy that pleasure-seeking and self-interest are the chief end of life, it should not be forgotten that happiness is an important item in Jesus' philosophy.

However, this distinction must be noted: Jesus teaches that happiness comes not by making it the chief quest of life but as the result of faithful stewardship. All the problems of pain and pleasure which occupied so large a place in the pagan philosophies are solved by Jesus' loyalty to the program of His Father. However heroic may be the demands of His stewardship, Jesus teaches that it was His "joy" and His "meat" to do the will of God.

> "O Joy that seekest me through pain,
>   I cannot close my heart to Thee;
> I trace the rainbow through the rain,
> And feel the promise is not vain
>   That morn shall tearless be."

This note of joy and victory is perhaps the most remarkable characteristic of the last hours of our Lord before He was swallowed up in the darkness of Calvary. John Wesley said, "Our people die well." Later he showed that he could do the same. But more than dying well is the promise of Jesus' words, "that your joy may be full." For none will die well unless first one has learned to live well. I think we were all thrilled during the days of the Great War by Alan Seeger's lines, sent home from France:

> "I have a rendezvous with death
>   At some disputed barricade
> When spring comes back with rustling shade."

But I, for one, was more thrilled by the lines, written later by a young high-school student:

> "I have a rendezvous with life
> In days I hope will come.
>
> .   .   .   .
>
> Though wet, nor blow, nor space I fear,
> Yet fear I deeply too,
> Lest death shall strike and claim me ere
> I keep Life's rendezvous."

Just so the joy promised by Jesus in today's scripture is a promise for the life that is here and now. When I was a boy in a Vermont school, we used to sing at morning chapel,

> "There's a song in the air every day in the year,
>   Though the sun shines hot or the wind blows cold,
> A song filling weary hearts with gladsome cheer,
>   A song that never, never can grow old."

I used to wonder during some very unhappy days where that song was to be found. But in after days I made the discovery. It may surprise some young people, but the fact is that real religion is the source of it—and the only source of it.

Recently I found a good story in the Southland. One of our Southern bishops is reported to have asked a fine-faced Negro, as the train stopped at a rural station, "Uncle, does anyone around here enjoy religion?" With twinkling eye "Uncle" replied, "Yes, sah, them that has it does, sah!" Of course the colored man's answer needs interpretation, but it was surely a great hour in my own experience when I looked out of the window of my room over the college football field and heard a Voice saying clearly to me, "I am come that they might have life, and ... have it more abundantly."

Oh, when will the world—yes, and the Church too—really come to discover that the Lord Jesus holds the key to joyous and victorious living? And yet we must always remember that joy is an inward experience and comes not by making it the chief quest of life but as a result of faithful attention, as the boy Jesus said, to "my Father's business."

* * *

A Prayer

O God, the day returns and brings a thousand joyous opportunities; help us to make the most of every one. Teach us to be glad. Grant that our eyes may all day long behold Thy blue; that every song of bird may find an echo in our hearts; or if the sky be overcast and gathering storms have hushed the notes of birds, grant that we then may draw from out the treasure store-house of our souls, and still be glad in Thee. Amen.

Meditation

"To do the work and seize the joy of each day as it comes, so that the forward look shall not dim our eyes to the beauty along the road; and to let the light of the Christ-revealed God fall on every scene and time, leading us to regard every touch of loveliness in earth and sky, every sweet affection and fellowship, every holy thought and aspiration as signs that behind all the mystery of this strange world there is a Great Heart of Love, in whose keeping we are safe!"—*W. Garrett Horder.*

Eternally Spring

I heard a bluebird in the field today
    Shouting aloud its springtime joy,
My heart leaped backward through the years
    And knelt before a laughing boy.

"O Boy," I prayed, "give back to me
  My laughter of that other day;
Give me the spirit, glad and free,
  That once I knew along the way."

He saw me not! Yet in his eye
  I read the answer to my plea:
"Joy lives not in the yesterdays,
  But in the living now," said he.

Seize thou the joy of every day,
  For gladness thrills the common sod,
And every brook and every bird
  May sing to you the joy of God!

CHAPTER THREE

Jesus Teaching Stewardship

I

REPENT—THE KINGDOM

"The kingdom of God is at hand: repent ye" (Mark 1. 15).

ACROSS centuries prophets have been crying, "Repent ye!" In the fullness of time when John the Baptist came he too cried, "Repent!" Then when the greatest Teacher of the ages arrived He began His ministry with the same appeal, "Repent! Repent! Repent!"

Why repent? Why this appeal of the centuries? Of course we know one basic answer: In our hearts we feel the need of repentance!

Who can come into the presence of God—in the sanctuary or in some other place—without feeling a sense of sin and unworthiness? We know what Peter felt when the holy life of Jesus overcame him, "Depart from me; for I am a sinful man," he cried.

Which psalm, outside of the twenty-third, do we repeat most often? Is it not the fifty-first? "Have mercy upon me, O God, according to thy lovingkindness: according to the multitude of thy tender mercies blot out my transgressions." In the depths of our souls we know why we need to repent!

But there must also be *another answer,* for Jesus came saying, "The kingdom of God is at hand: Repent ye." Certainly in Jesus' mind repentance was necessary not only because of our personal relation to God but also because of our relation to God's kingdom and its consummation here on earth.

Henry Ward Beecher once told of a little girl who interrupted her prayer at her mother's knee to ask, "Mama, what is God doing all day long?" The child had begun to think! It had occurred to her that God really must have greater business even than keeping little children and other good folk safe during the night. If the Church, from the beginning, had clearly grasped Jesus' message and program, it is doubtful if any little girl anywhere would have to ask such a question of her mother.

Jesus is saying here at the very beginning of His ministry, "The time has now come, God's reign is near: repent and believe the gospel" (Moffatt).

Is this not a call *to repent of our Kingdom sins—our sins that have stalled the coming of the Kingdom, that have made us indifferent to the reign of God on earth?* Indifferent to the heartaches of our neighbors? Indifferent to the higher welfare of the nation? Unconcerned about the condition of the peoples of the whole wide world? How we need to repent!

Now, John the Baptist, who was Jesus' forerunner, preached this very kind of Kingdom repentance:

" 'Make the way ready for the Lord,

.   .   .   .

the crooked made straight, the rough roads smooth.'

.   .   .   .

"Now, produce fruits that answer to your repentance" (Luke 3. 4, 5, 8, Moffatt).

Under the intense earnestness of John the people asked, "What are we to do?"

If we will carefully read John's words, we shall realize that every one of his answers was a command to them to straighten out the social and moral relationships with their fellows. Upon this kind of repentance were the people to secure not only the forgiveness of men, but that deeper need, the forgiveness of God.

Jesus' messages abound with this kind of teaching. Why do we neglect such commands as He gave in the Sermon on the Mount? He said, "If you remember, even when offering your gift at the altar, that your brother has any grievance against you, leave your gift at the very altar and go away; first be reconciled to your brother, then come back and offer your gift."

Perhaps the thing about Jesus that gave most surprise was His love for people. "Wherever he saw the multitude he had compassion on them." Oh, how much we need the stewardship of the tender heart! "He that loveth not his brother whom he hath seen, how can he love God whom he hath not seen?" (1 John 4. 20.)

* * *

A Prayer

Dear God, enlarge our hearts, we pray. Our vision is so narrow and our sympathies so dwarfed. May Thy Spirit Presence help us to widen our horizons this very day; and may we begin at home. In Jesus' name. Amen.

Meditation

"Life is a stewardship; this is the teaching of Jesus Christ. Fundamentally, this teaching throughout the Scriptures is based on God's ownership, both by creation and redemption. Thus, stewardship becomes the Christian interpretation of life, and is concerned with

the Christian's use of all the resources committed to
him, of possessions, of personality, of prayer."—*Methodist Discipline,* Paragraph 168.

Blindness

I do not know how selfish eyes
Make clouds in heaven's skies;
But I do know, where'er I go,
That it is so!

I do not know how hasty words that start
Unconquered from my selfish heart,
Return to me their bitter smart;
But that it's so
I know, I know!

I do not know how as I pass men by,
With careless gaze and hardened eye,
Something within me starts to die;
But that it's so
I know, I know!

I do not know why war or hate or greed
Has always failed the human need,
Become at length a broken reed;
But that it's so
I know, I know!

Dear God, it must be Thou hast made it so,
For always, wheresoe'er I go,
Two things, in light or dark, I find:
Eternal Love before, behind;
And that my sin will make me blind!
That this is so, I know, I know!

II

USELESS AND MISERABLE

"Make me as one of thy hired servants" (Luke 15. 19).

"Oh, I feel so useless!" Then the young woman
threw herself into a luxurious chair as she added, "And
I'm so miserable!"

Is there any connection between being useless and being miserable? Someone should write the story of the prodigal daughter. Such a story would begin not with ugly vice, but with downright uselessness. *Jesus taught that a sense of stewardship is necessary to the peace and happiness of "the good steward" himself.*

But we can't judge the young woman who was "useless" and "miserable" unless we know her environment. Who has not observed these two kinds of mothers? The one who patted the head of her little daughter, as the little girl industriously washed the dishes, and said to the neighbor: "I don't know how I could get along without my little helper. I told her father last night that I couldn't keep house without Jane."

Another mother said: "Now, Mary, you go and get right after the dishes. It won't take you long, and then you can play. Now, go on!" And Mary went, but not without saying, "Oh, I hate dishes!"

Blessed is the child whose mother or father knows how to teach him that the joy of life comes not from having something done for you but in doing for someone else. This was the lesson that the prodigal son had to learn.

Jesus said that the prodigal *"came to himself."* In the language of modern youth, when the prodigal waked up, he found himself "a flop"—just plain "useless." That is the explanation of these words, "I will arise and go to my father, and I will say unto him—" Say what? Watch the words, "I have sinned against heaven and in thy sight, and am no more worthy to be called thy son." Yes, these words are all there; but the key words—the words that reveal the character of his repentance—are these two words that followed—

"Make me." Make me what? "Make me something! Something that I now am not. Make me a servant—anything that's of some use in the world." This is what the prodigal said, and that was an awakening indeed.

But we will not see how great an awakening it was until we contrast those two words, "Make me," with two other words which he used on a former occasion when he said to his father, "Give me." How often those words, "Give me," have been used across the years, even in our day!

Some time ago a Chicago newspaper printed, as a striking cartoon, an empty hand extended in appeal. On the hand was printed the words, "Gimme!" and underneath it was labeled, "The American Relief Map." Of course that cartoon doesn't tell the whole story. It does great wrong to many hard-working people who are the victims of our social and economic sins. And yet when I see Colfax Street in Denver blocked before the moving-picture theater on "Bank Night" or "Auto Night," and witness the throngs of human beings with their eyes bulging and their hands out, hoping to get something for nothing, I feel a shame for my fellow Americans which I wish they might feel for themselves.

Moreover, I pray that all of us may more deeply learn the lesson of the prodigal, which is that the satisfactions of life come not from the "Give me" attitude, but from the awakened heart which day after day says, "Father, make me."

"For life is the mirror of king and of slave,
    'Tis just what we are and do.
Give to the world the best you have,
    And the best will come back to you."

A Prayer

Gracious Father, help me this day to be aware of the needs of others. They are just as hungry as I am; they need as I do some word of encouragement, some expression of human interest. Let me be Thy messenger today. I pray in Jesus' name. Amen.

Meditation

"So long as we love, we serve; so long as we are loved by others, I would almost say that we are indispensable; and no man is useless while he has a friend."
—*Robert Louis Stevenson*.

Under an Apple Tree

If Thou canst make so wonderful
  This thrilling thing, a tree,
I wonder, Lord, what Thou couldst make
  If man should yield to Thee;

If every tiny earth-born root
  Drank from the wells of God,
If all day long his every breath
  Answered Thy slightest nod?

Bent, twisted, gnarled, time-eaten,
  But a glorious thing this tree,
With hands and heart uplifted
  Seeking the face of Thee!

O Thou who made so wondrous fair
  This thrilling thing, my tree,
Because its every hour is lived
  An offering unto Thee,

Oh, take me, root and branch and all
  (The years go on apace!),
Grow up in me that radiant life
  That shines, Lord, from Thy face!

III

SQUINT-EYED PEOPLE

"These ye ought to have done, and not to have left the other undone" (Matthew 23. 23, A. R. V.).

Jesus taught that a good steward must see things clearly, and see them whole. And he must be able to distinguish the "means" from the "ends," and to see the importance of both.

But some people are squint-eyed; they can't see more than one thing at a time. We ought to be very sorry for such folks, and we ought to be very patient with them too. For it may be that we ourselves are a bit squint-eyed on some subjects. Most people are. For instance, some unknown person writes,

> "They may not need me, yet they might;
> I'll let my heart be just in sight—
> A smile so small as mine may be
> Precisely their necessity!"

Now, some people will exclaim: "Good! That is religion indeed!" No, that is only a part of religion. Think it over carefully. Kindness and mercy, as Jesus taught us in our previous study, are badly needed in this world of ours. But how long would "kindness" last if people should stop kneeling down before the Source of kindness? Our point is that *kindliness and worship must go together*. And what God has joined together we have no business to put asunder.

On the other hand it is a strange thing that there are so many squint-eyed people, like the Pharisees, who were very careful about their kneeling down—about the means and methods of worship—yet who never seemed to learn to love mercy and kindness toward

their fellow men. What great progress it would have
meant if those very precise churchmen had gotten
saturated with the threefold content of that great and
grand Old Testament statement, "What doth the Lord
require of thee, but to do justly, and to love mercy,
and to walk humbly with thy God?"

Not justice *or* mercy *or* worship is specified! It is
not either this or that, or any two of them. It is all
three of them that must be observed if we are to be
pleasing unto God.

So while it is very easy for us to criticize these
Pharisees in today's scripture and call them "squint-
eyed hypocrites," and say, "They saw only the forms
and commandments of religion; they never got to the
heart of it," are we so sure that we have gotten either
to the heart of it, or even to the outside of it?

Take the matter of tithing, for example. Its purpose was to make good stewards of God, to help man
to remember that God is the owner and giver of all
things. When they brought the first fruits of the
soil and the firstlings of the flocks, it was to acknowledge His lovingkindness and to pay a debt of gratitude
to the Creator of all. And it worked! It was an efficient means to the great end of making God real. The
fact that some people, like those Pharisees, became
blind to the purposes and the ends of tithing, and so
worshiped the thing itself, is no excuse for us to neglect
this means of grace.

Jesus said: "Woe unto you, hypocrites. You are
very precise; you pay tithes even of your garden vege-
tables, and then you omit the weightier matters of
justice and mercy and faith." Of course we can add our
condemnation of their failures in justice and mercy;
but why do we forget that when Jesus said of justice

and mercy, "These ought ye to have done," He also said of their tithing and holy habits, "Don't leave these undone"?

Well, which side of the question are we going to squint at—this side or that side? Why not listen to Jesus? He says, "It is not either this side or that side: it is both this *and* that side."

Oh, how lopsided we are prone to become unless we constantly keep our eyes and ears on "the sweet reasonableness of Jesus"! The early Church had its controversy over "faith and works." We have been having ours over the social gospel and the gospel for the individual. And always there are those who will discuss whether it is "tithing" or "stewardship." As if any truly good steward can carelessly discard the experience of the centuries. "What therefore God hath joined together, let not man put asunder."

* * *

A Prayer

O Lord, my Lord, "how excellent is Thy name in all the earth"! Best of all, how excellent is Thy name in my own heart! Abide with me this day; so shall my every labor be a song, and from my life shall come a strength to cheer the comrades of my toil. Make me the steward of Thy grace today for Jesus' sake. Amen.

Meditation

"It seems incredible that men, confessing themselves redeemed and regenerated, are still debating the obligations of stewardship. It cannot be that they who find their chief satisfaction in adding to their hoardings, and who pinch all they owe to God into a tithe and the tithe into a pittance, realize how desperate is their trifling with God and their own souls."—*Bishop Earl Cranston.*

My Creed

I hold such creeds to be earth-bound and futile,
    Vain breathings of a sentimental clod,
That fail to turn the face to Christ the Saviour,
    Or point a hungry heart to God.

I also would be true for those who trust me,
    And I too would be pure, and strong and brave;
But how be all of this, or friend to friendless,
    While heedless of the One who died to save?

My heart is hungry for a Presence,
    Some Living One to lift me from the sod;
My creed must tell of more than human doings,
    My creed must lift my lonely heart to God!

IV

SILLY, IS IT?

"And for their sakes I sanctify myself" (John 17. 19).

"But that seems silly!"

It was a young lady who thus spoke to the parson. The preacher winced a bit, but he kept his poise. He knew this modern youth. He respected her strength of mind and will, even if sometimes he differed with her standards.

That afternoon his automobile had been ticketed for overparking. He had told her about it; then had said: "I deserved the ticket. It was one hour parking. I didn't intend to leave it so long. It was my carelessness; I ought to pay."

Then it was that the girl exploded: "But that seems silly. As for me, I watch the police and get away with two hours of parking when I can. And so do others."

"But don't you see I wish to be a good citizen?" the preacher interrupted. "The parking laws were made to keep order in the city. I feel a sort of stewardship at that point. Don't you see?"

But young America didn't see; and all the parson could do was to say, "Well, I feel a little disappointed in you. But," he added, "perhaps I have an exaggerated sense of responsibility." Was the parson right or wrong?

Next, how about that football star, who last fall was expelled from a well-known college team because he would smoke and would occasionally drink, against the rules? Were the coaches "silly" or the player?

And that trustee of one of our Eastern churches who was requested to resign from the official board because he sold liquor in his restaurant, how about that?

I recall the earnestness with which one of the so-called "godless" youth of Russia said to our group in Moscow, "Our organization is fighting three things, sex impurity, liquor, and tobacco."

When someone asked, "Why are you fighting these things?" the reply was, "We young people can't afford to waste our money or our health when we have on our hands the job of making a new Russia."

Perhaps it was something like that which made Saint Paul to say, "If meat make my brother to offend, I will eat no flesh while the world standeth." This tireless battler for Christ had been asked as to the rightness or wrongness of a Christian's eating the meat which had been offered to idols as part of the pagan religious ceremony of the day.

Paul answered, "An idol is as nothing to me. It

doesn't hurt my conscience. But if I have a brother, for whom Christ died, who is hurt by my example, I'll quit eating. For I have a stewardship! My big business is to help Christ make a Christian world. Nothing shall interfere with that!"

What a difference it would make in the Church of Jesus Christ today if we could get every member to feel as Paul did—"I have a stewardship."

A few minutes ago this train, on which I am riding through Wyoming, stopped at a small station. Then something interesting happened. A mother dog stood with her woolly puppy in a yard near the railroad tracks. The mother herself was young enough to start several times to run and bark at our train. But she looked at her puppy and stayed in the yard.

Finally, as our train moved ahead, the dog rushed out toward the tracks. But when she reached the edge of a six-foot embankment she abruptly stopped. She could easily have made the jump herself, but the puppy couldn't. With a look at her offspring she turned back to a road some forty feet away, where the puppy could safely follow.

Now, if a dog will do things like that for her puppy's sake, what ought a good steward of the mysteries of God do for the Kingdom's sake? Holiness for its own sake easily becomes wooden and unreal. It is when holiness and a great "cause" are tied up together that both become mighty. "For their sakes I sanctify myself."

* * *

A Prayer

Another day is here, dear Lord, another day of service for Thy kingdom and for Thee. Help us to be strong. If we are tempted to be weak, grant us Thy strength. And if sometimes the hours seem dull and we are tempted to grow weary in well-doing, at such times show us the power and the glory and the challenge of the cross. Amen.

Meditation

"Self-sacrifice is an everyday affair. By it we live. Without it society could not go on for an hour. . . . I mean by self-sacrifice any diminution of my possessions, pleasures or powers, in order to increase those of others. . . . The greatest conceivable sacrifice is when I give myself."—*Palmer.*

Introspection

What care I who gets the credit?
　Only let the work be done!
Christ Himself will handle credits
　With the setting of the sun,

Praise or blame, what does it matter?
　Rise above them every day;
Soul, you'll never win a battle
　If you fear what men may say.

Keep your eye on God, ye preacher,
　People praise and people blame,
Sometimes cheer and sometimes curse you,
　Do your duty just the same.

While the world is sick and waiting
　For the something I can be,
Help me, Lord, in stress and struggle
　Just to keep my eyes on Thee.

V

God's Ownership

"O that men would praise the Lord for his goodness, and for his wonderful works to the children of men!" (Psalm 107. 31).

This is the psalm of thanksgiving. It begins with an exhortation, "O give thanks unto the Lord." And then it proceeds to tell us why we should. It is really an ancient and better edition of the modern song,

"Count your many blessings, name them one by one,
  And it will surprise you what the Lord hath done!"

It surely is an impressive list of blessings which the psalmist enumerates. After each of the five sections, like a hallelujah chorus, he repeats the noble words,

"O that men would praise the Lord for his goodness,
  And for his wonderful works to the children of men!"

This scripture has an important bearing upon our stewardship studies because it helps to interpret *Jesus' teaching that man's stewardship obligation rests upon God's ownership*. We belong to God, therefore we should do God's work. We belong to Him because He created us. More than that, we belong to God because He has redeemed us. As Saint Paul says, "Know ye not that . . . ye are not your own? For ye are bought with a price" (1 Corinthians 6. 19, 20).

But the stewardship obligation is more than any legal obligation. According to Jesus, our God is a Father who has loved us with an everlasting love.

Thus gratitude to God compels the faithful steward to rise above legalism and to sing gratefully,

> "Were the whole realm of nature mine,
>   That were an offering far too small.
> Love so amazing, so divine,
>   Demands my soul, my life, my all."

But our big difficulty in this regard is to feel that there is actual reality in Jesus' teaching of God's fundamental ownership of life. In this busy and materialistic world it is not easy.

"For every beast of the forest *is* mine, *and* the cattle upon a thousand hills," saith the Lord; but the cattlemen can't see it as easily as the poet or the prophet does. Nor does the farmer easily think of crop-raising as a partnership with God. Oh, that he might! What he does remember is how he worked in the sweat of his brow. In the sanctuary we can sing with lusty thoughtlessness,

> "All things come of Thee, O God,
>   And of Thine own have we given Thee,"

but on Monday, when we get into the competition of the market place, we are prone to be "more practical"!

Thus a magazine article tells of an excited manufacturer who exclaimed as he was confronted with a strike among his workmen, "I am just childish enough to believe that what is mine is my own; and that when my old dad turned over to me this mill, along with his gold watch and the old family horse, he meant that I should do with it just as I pleased."

Of course such an attitude, if persisted in, pretty much rules God out of the picture, just as it rules out any real appreciation of Christian stewardship. As an English writer sums it up, "It makes a vast difference in the long run whether a man has at the back of his mind, in all his judgments, the pagan principle, 'One has a right to do as one likes with one's own,' or, on the other hand, the idea of property as a social trust or stewardship. Change of attitude here is the most practical thing that can happen to men."

It seems, therefore, that our great need is to study Jesus' teaching concerning God's actual ownership of life and property and all. At least sixteen of His parables reveal His emphasis upon this fundamental doctrine. And yet here is one of the most stubbornly resisted truths of the Scriptures.

But let a person once see this truth and realize its practical implications, and God not only becomes a Presence personal and real, but the entire conception of one's relation to all industry and to the kingdom of God is revolutionized. "O that men would praise the Lord for his goodness, and for his wonderful works to the children of men!"

* * *

A Prayer

Dear Heavenly Father, grant us wisdom and guidance for this day. Thou hast created us and redeemed us. Thy love is from everlasting to everlasting; we would rest in Thee. Grant that all our resources, of mind and heart and will, may be dedicated anew this day to the advancement of Thy kingdom. Through Jesus Christ our Lord. Amen.

Meditation

"Therefore as every man is wholly God's own portion by the title of creation, so all our labors and care, all our powers and faculties must be wholly employed in the service of God, and even all the days of our life; that this life being ended, we may live with him forever."—*Jeremy Taylor*.

At Evening

O what a world is this,
A world of beauty and of stars!
How did you make it, God?
And who and what are You?
How do you reach my heart,
And stir my mind
With questions such as these?
Yea, and what am I
To look upon Thy loveliness?
So beautiful this sky!

How did you do it, God?
Those rapturous clouds,
That skyline underneath,
Silver- and gold-streaked,
Those changing colors, and
The wistful mountains,
Majestic, purple, white?
And oh, that evening star!
Thanks for the stars;
O what a world is this!

And, God, what is this hunger
Gnawing in my heart?
Where are you, Mighty One?
What is this whisp'ring voice,
Insistent, sweet and low?
Dear God, it must be,
Thou art nearer,
Nearer than we know.
Oh, in my hungry heart,
I pray it may be so!

VI

GUESTS OF GOD

"You are only guests of mine, passing wayfarers" (Leviticus 25. 23, Moffatt).

Yes, there are "practical" difficulties in the way of making real the stewardship statement, "God is the owner of all things." But across the entire Old Testament times the Lord and His prophets have been trying to overcome this difficulty.

For instance, like a flash of illumination comes Doctor Moffatt's translation of Leviticus 25. 23. Jehovah is saying to his Israel, "No land is to be sold in perpetuity, for the land is mine, and you are only guests of mine, passing wayfarers." Guests of God! How true that is! Why can't all men see it? And Jesus, the Supreme Teacher, based His stewardship message on this solid foundation: Ye are guests of God.

To this end Jesus painted His parable pictures. The prodigal son was doubly a sinner because he was wasting not his own but his father's substance (Luke 15). In the story of the unjust steward "a certain rich man," whose property is being wasted, is suggestive of God (Luke 16). The householder who went out at dawn to hire workmen for his vineyard is another picture which Jesus draws of the Lord of all workmen (Matthew 20). Nor will we forget that parable of the supreme Householder, the Lord of all the earth, who made a vineyard and "let it out to vinedressers" who should care for it (Matthew 21). All these parables, and others, are intended to underscore the big question, Who owns the earth and all that is therein? God answers, "You are only guests of mine, passing wayfarers."

Really, there is nothing impractical or unreal about the Scripture teachings of God's ownership of all things. Once a friend wrote asking me to preach on "Our Debt to the Past" at the one hundredth anniversary of his church.

I was at our summer cottage on the shore of Seneca Lake. Meditatingly I said to myself as I walked out of doors, "What do we owe to the past?" The first thing I saw was a tree. "We certainly owe that to the past. It takes a long time to grow a tree," I mused.

> "Poems are made by fools like me,
> But only God can make a tree."

Then that set me to meditating on how much we owe to the poets and writers of the past, and there came rushing through my mind wonderful quotations from David's time clear down through Shakespeare and Browning and Charles Wesley.

It was a glorious summer day and as I stopped in my meditation under the trees, I happened to look up and caught a glimpse of my dear old mother-in-love, sitting on the piazza and enjoying meditations of her own.

And that set me going again! How much we owe to our homes. Yes, and to the much criticized mother-in-law. How else can we figure it out—we who appreciate our wives?

And what about our debt to country? How much we owe to our Pilgrim fathers and mothers who landed on a "rock-bound coast," seeking God. And those fathers and mothers who prayed and worked for independence and freedom?

Some modern historians will tell us that it never happened in Philadelphia. There never was an old man in the belfry and a little boy down on the street, crying, "Ring, grandpa, ring! Oh, ring for liberty!"

Never mind! Our fathers and mothers were there! And they did say with tense voices as they waited in front of that historic building: "Will they do it? Dare they do it? What of Adams? What of Sherman? Oh, God grant they won't refuse!"

Today we face new issues here in America. Perhaps greater issues than our fathers and mothers knew at any time. It helps me to face these issues patiently and with sacrificial spirit if I say to myself, "What hast thou that thou hast not received?" I repeat over to myself those matchless words of Abraham Lincoln, "Four score and seven years ago our fathers brought forth upon this continent a new nation. . . . It is . . . for us to be here dedicated to . . . that cause for which they here gave the last full measure of devotion. . . ."

Well, the result of my meditations that morning was a revelation to me, our debt to the past included about everything I could think of, even our mothers-in-law. But clearest of all there stood out *one supreme fact. That is the fact of Christ.* He, more than any other, has made this world a livable world.

Let me end this study where I began it, at the little summer cottage on the shore of Seneca Lake. I well remember the stewardship lesson taught me on the very day when that little place came into our own possession. My teacher was the farmer who had lived there and had come to love every foot of the soil. As we came to the moment when he was to pass to me the papers, he paused. His eyes wandered lovingly over the pasture, the garden, the glen, the shoreline of the lake.

Then he said to me, "I have put a lot of work into

this place. There is one thing I would like to have you understand. I wouldn't think of selling it to you *if I thought you would let it run down."*

It occurred to me that God has put a lot into His world; that His Son has given His life for it; that His prophets and His saints have put more into it than we can conceive. All of this has been given us as a heritage, as guests of God. How much we owe Him!

* * *

A Prayer

Dear God, how wonderful is Thy gift of life! Give us grateful hearts this day lest we forget. If we are tempted to complain, help us then to enumerate our blessings. As we journey on, help us to ease the burden of some weaker soul. So may we spread abroad Thy joy. In Jesus' name. Amen.

Meditation

"It is indeed a remarkable fact that suffering and hardships do not, as a rule, abate the love of life: They seem, on the contrary, to give it a keener zest."—*William James.*

Sheer Joy

O the sheer joy of it,
  Living with Thee,
God of the universe,
  Lord of a tree,
Maker of mountains,
  Lover of me!

O the sheer joy of it,
  Breathing Thy air;
Morning is dawning,
  Gone every care,
All the world's singing,
  God's everywhere.

O the sheer joy of it,
  Walking with Thee,
Out by the hilltop,
  Down by the sea,
Life is so wonderful,
  Life is so free!

O the sheer joy of it,
  Working with God,
Running His errands,
  Waiting His nod,
Building His heaven,
  On common sod.

O the sheer joy of it,
  Ever to be,
Living in glory,
  Living with Thee,
Lord of tomorrow,
  Lover of me!

VII

PUFFED-UP PEOPLE

"Now some are puffed up" (1 Corinthians 4. 18).

If there are "practical" difficulties in the way of
recognizing God's ownership, there are also practical
results of not doing it. Sometimes these results are
pathetic; sometimes they would be funny if they were
not so tragic.

Some years ago, in the old historic state of Massachusetts, we had a neighbor. I did not get acquainted
with her until she learned that my ancestors must have
been acquainted with her ancestors during a stormy
passage across the Atlantic in that ever-growing ship,
the *Mayflower*. Then she sought us out!

After that, wherever we met, there was just one subject of conversation—an ancient ship and an ancient
people. One day she confided to me that after going

over her genealogy again, she found that she was thirty times descended from the Pilgrim fathers and mothers. What a descent!

Now, I have sometimes wondered what Saint Paul would have said to a sister like that one. I have wondered too what she did with those words of the apostle, "forgetting the things which are behind" (Philippians 3. 13). And I have wondered because I never knew her to be interested in anything that had to do with the making of a better neighborhood, a better nation, or a better world; and she possessed both talent and time and this world's goods.

"Forgetting the things which are behind" is splendid advice. Sometimes! What did Paul mean by those words? Just this: *Remembering the past generally does one of two things to people. It will either make you a steward of God, with a passion to use what the past has given you, or it will make you a puffed-up person, the object of laughter on earth and tears in heaven.*

Why is this so? Harvey Reeves Calkins phrased an unforgettable truth when he said, "To have is to owe." This was what Saint Paul was thinking too when he wrote to those puffed-up Corinthians, "What hast thou that thou didst not receive?" (1 Corinthians 4. 7.)

Picture this strong church in Corinth, with its official board rebelling at some of the suggestions and requests which the apostle had made. They said some rather uncomplimentary things about Paul. "Why should we continue to take orders from this traveling preacher?"

In a tender, but very pointed letter Paul replies something like this: "Some years ago an itinerant preacher stopped off in your town and preached the gospel. Around him gathered a little band of praying men and women. Through great persecution and by real sacrifice that preacher and that little group of faithful souls laid the foundation of a church. That church is now yours."

And Paul continues, "Perhaps you have a right to be independent, but first I want you to consider one question, 'What hast thou that thou didst not receive?' Where would your church be if it had not been for the fathers and mothers who gathered around that itinerant preacher, whom some of you would now despise?"

I think we would all walk humbly if we could only keep before us *our debt to the past.* See that business man who pats himself on the back, saying: "This is my business; I built it. I can do as I please with my own." How ignorant he is!

Now, Jesus built one of His stewardship parables around this kind of a man. History has called him "The Rich Fool." But don't let us think that what made him a fool was his riches. That only helped. What made him a fool was his answer to the question, "Who is the owner of the earth and all therein?"

The fool replied, "I am the owner of all I can get my hands on." And he got his hands on much. Not merely because he was skillful, but because *"the ground brought forth plentifully."*

Then, instead of saying, "I have a stewardship," and giving thanks to the Creator of all, he said, "I have much goods laid up for many years, I will take mine ease, eat, drink and be merry."

"But God said unto him, Thou fool, this night thy soul shall be required of thee; then whose shall those things be?" (Luke 12. 20.) Thus Jesus taught, in vivid parable, the eternal truth that God is the owner of all things.

A Prayer

"O God, our help in ages past,
Our hope for years to come,
Be Thou our guide while life shall last,
And our eternal home!" Amen.

Meditation

We laugh at little Jack Horner, who "put in his thumb and drew out a plum" from the pie he did not make, and cried, "What a big boy am I!" But, after all, there is not a very great distance between the childishness of that small boy and that of the grown-up child who gloats over what *he* "owns" and what *he* has done, "all myself"—all the while deaf to the Voice which says, "What hast thou that thou didst not receive?"

At Lake Louise

When first I saw thy emerald waters, Lake Louise,
And felt the awe of majesty that round thee lies,
That glacier gleaming, and on either side,
Those noble heights that rise
Encircling, jagged, green, beneath blue skies,
The world stood hushed—one only sound,
A bird that dared to sing on holy ground!

. . . .

Who would not lift his heart in thankfulness to God
For eyes to see and feet to walk such sod?

CHAPTER FOUR

Stewards of the Cross

I

NEW FOUNDATIONS

"For the love of Christ constraineth us" (2 Corinthians 5. 14).

> "In the cross of Christ I glory,
> Towering o'er the wrecks of time."

GOOD poetry; but vastly more! These lines from the well-known hymn tell of the historic truth: Christ and His Cross tower above the wrecks of time. And there have been many wrecks; and more are to follow.

In the preceding chapter we have seen how Jesus builded His teaching concerning stewardship squarely upon the foundation of God's ownership. But here we have something more. In the Cross of Christ is a new basis for loyalty to the Kingdom and the King.

We have seen that no man, whether loyal or disloyal, will ever be able to get away from his duty as a steward of God. "For we must all appear before the judgment seat of Christ" (2 Corinthians 5. 10). But at Calvary the basis of stewardship is lifted to a higher level. It is the level of love. There, at the Cross of Christ, the Creator is seen in a new light; He is the Redeemer, the Lord of Love!

> "Lord of all being, throned afar,
> Thy glory flames from sun and star;
> Center and soul of every sphere,
> Yet to each loving heart how near!"

Repeat that last line, "Yet to each loving heart how near!" Yes, since Calvary "the Lord of all being" has been the Redeemer of men. Therefore the call to stewardship has been based upon a new foundation. Love now gives a new meaning to duty, that the two may walk hand in hand in victorious stewardship!

So the stewardship obligation has not decreased but rather increased, and a new eagerness has taken possession of the good steward. Now there is a new motive, of grateful love—love that has been surveying "the wondrous cross." But we should mark the apostle's words that the love of Christ not merely does something *for* him but does something *to* him. "Constraineth us" is the phrase he uses. It means action. He might have said, "The love of Christ compels me to get into action." So there is no lessening of the sense of duty, rather a quickening.

And this is because a sense of duty is basic in the making of life strong and beautiful and Christian. One of Jesus' great sayings in the Sermon on the Mount was, "Think not that I am come to destroy the law, or the prophets: I am not come to destroy, but to fulfill."

Too often we find persons who seem to think that they can make love a substitute for duty. As Gipsy Smith once said, "You can preach love in such a way that people can get lovesick." But the love that dominates the Sermon on the Mount is truly the fulfillment of duty. "The love of Christ constraineth me," is another way of saying, "I have a stewardship."

John Wesley evidently had the stewardship of the Cross in his mind when he put on his private seal the three words, "Believe—Obey—Love." These words not only summarize Wesley's experience but really indicate the secret of the victorious life. To truly "believe" in the Cross of Christ marks the beginning. "Love" is the climax. But "Obey" holds the others together. There can be no progress in faith without obedience.

> "Walk in the light, so shalt thou know
> That fellowship of love."

Joyce Kilmer, who met an untimely death on a French battlefield, has made very clear what Paul meant in today's scripture. The sufferings of our Lord were so real to the poet, that his own suffering is made easy. He writes,

> "My shoulders ache beneath my pack,
> (Lie easier, cross, upon His back.)
> My rifle hand is stiff and numb,
> (From Thy pierced palm red rivers come!)"

And then these immortal words:

> "Lord, Thou didst suffer more for me
> Than all the hosts of land and sea.
> So let me render back again
> This millionth of Thy gift. Amen."

* * *

A Prayer

Hold Thou Thy Cross, dear Lord, this day before our waking eyes. We would not wait until youth is gone and manhood's strength is dying; give us now courage to fight the good fight. Grant us victory this day we pray, in Thy dear name. Amen.

Meditation

"Christianity, he saw, was not what he did for God, but what God did in him. Of course Wesley understood that an inner experience which did not turn into outer action would stultify itself. So his inner experience became a program of action which involved an organization. However, it was primarily a new vitality. It related itself to every issue of human life. But, first of all, it was a fountain of energy playing in a man's soul."—*Lynn Harold Hough.*

A Morning Meditation

I

The morning sun is on the treetops,
   The morning bird is on the wing,
The morning peace falls on my spirit,
   God's splendor lies on everything.

Then, like an ugly shadow, darkening
   The hills and valley where the glory lay,
Comes to my mind the fever and the fretting,
   The irritating duties of this day.

Oh, could I ever rest here on my hilltop,
   Far from life's struggle in a rich release,
Oh, could I ever hold this fragrance from the garden,
   So might I keep alive this morning peace!

II

Nay, O my Soul, beware this vain delusion!
   Peace is not resting on some quiet hill,
Peace does not come to those a-fleeing
   The trampled fields where battle rages still;

Peace is the joy of hearts that struggle,
   That face life's battles when the bugles sound,
Peace is not living in secluded gardens
   Where roses and tranquillity abound;

Nay, peace comes not from morning sky-birds winging,
   Nor from the grander glory of the sun,
But, like sweet evening music softly falling,
   Peace is reward for daily duties done!

II

WHY FOOLISHNESS?

"For the preaching of the cross is to them that perish foolishness" (1 Corinthians 1. 18).

A few years ago at Northfield—not far from Round Top, wherein rest the ashes of Dwight L. Moody— one who knew the great business-man evangelist intimately sought to tell a group of us the "four secrets" of his success.

Here is one of the four; it is very simple. He said, "Moody preached the gospel—not good advice, but the good gospel of Christ." I think the preacher successfully pointed out that there is a difference between "good advice" and "the gospel." It is necessary, of course, that we should give good advice, but pity the preacher who fails to keep the gospel—the good news from God—central in all his preaching.

Long before Moody's time a still greater evangelist made a similar assertion, "For Christ sent me . . . to preach the gospel," he said; "not with the wisdom of words, lest the cross of Christ should be made of none effect." Evidently, "the cross" and "the gospel" were linked together in the mind of Saint Paul. And he preached them together, even though "the preaching of the cross is to them that perish foolishness" (1 Corinthians 1. 18).

Why foolishness? Why is the crucified Christ a stumbling block? Evidently, some very "wise" people had said to the evangelist: "Paul, you would get a better hearing for your preaching if you would stop talking about 'the Cross.' It is like waving a red flag in front of the Jews, and it is foolishness to philosophers

like the Greeks. Why don't you major on the life of
Jesus rather than upon his death?"

Why not? "You don't understand what you are
asking," Saint Paul answered. "You would drop out
the very heart of my gospel." "God forbid that I
should glory, save in the cross of our Lord Jesus Christ"
(Galatians 6. 14).

And there was a reason. Saint Paul had found it.
The Cross of Christ was not only the climax of the
Christ-life, but it was God's offering for man's sin.
John the Baptist had seen this when he pointed to
Jesus and said, "Behold the Lamb of God, which tak-
eth away the sin of the world." Moreover, that death
on the cross was the supreme appeal of the God of
Love.

> "Dear dying Lamb, Thy precious blood
>   Shall never lose its power,
> Till all the ransomed Church of God
>   Be saved, to sin no more."

But not many Jewish churchmen nor Greek scholars
would come. They would not accept God's Saviour.
They didn't need Him! "We are not sinners like the
Gentiles," the Jews replied, "we have Abraham for our
father." They were going to be saved by their ancestry
plus their religious traditions. And the philosophers
were going to be saved by their philosophy. It is still
so. The "blood theology" is still either a stumbling
block or a foolishness to many.

Most of us have never realized how terribly blinding
are the so-called respectable sins. They blind the eyes
against God; they shut out eternal life; they prevent
the coming of the Kingdom. We need a new realiza-
tion of the sinfulness of sin!

"On Calvary," said Kagawa at Madras, "I see the

blood of Jesus dropping down from His body onto the cross! I hear the sound of the agony of the Lamb of God for the sins of mankind! It was for me and for my nation and for my race and for the whole world! I have committed sins, and Jesus died for my sake! My race has committed sins, and He died for my race. And the whole of mankind has fallen into sin, so He died for us all."

Foolishness? Only those can so speak of the Cross who are perishing, whose eyes are blinded to Jesus' monumental words, "God loved the world so dearly that He gave up His only Son" (Moffatt).

* * *

A Prayer

Dear God, show us that we cannot love Thee unless we hate evil. May Thy Cross reveal to us more and more the depths of our own unworthiness and the everlasting mercy of our Lord and Saviour Jesus Christ. Amen.

Meditation

"We do not presume to come to this Thy table, O merciful Lord, trusting in our own righteousness, but in Thy manifold and great mercies. We are not worthy so much as to gather up the crumbs under Thy table. But Thou art the same Lord, whose property is always to have mercy. Grant us, therefore, gracious Lord, so to eat the flesh of Thy dear Son Jesus Christ, and to drink His blood, that we may live and grow thereby; and that, being washed through His most precious blood, we may evermore dwell in Him, and He in us. Amen."—*The Prayer Book.*

Calling

I have heard it in the mountains,
  I have heard it by the sea,
Where the plains are vast and vaster
I have heard it calling, calling,
  Ever calling unto me!

In the nighttime I have heard it
  Through the darkness and the gloom,
In the morning when the sunrise
  Bursts in splendor through my room.

Oh, what is it that is calling
  In the mountains, by the sea,
In the nighttime, in the daytime,
  Ever calling unto me?

            .   .   .   .   .

Oh, my soul, and can it be
It is God, and He is calling,
  Ever calling unto me!

III

CROSS-BEARING

"I lay down my life. . . . No man taketh it from me, but
I lay it down of myself" (John 10. 17, 18).

> "Must Jesus bear the cross alone,
>   And all the world go free?
> No, there's a cross for everyone,
>   And there's a cross for me."

But what do we know about cross-bearing? We
sing about it, and we repeat scripture about it; but
have we ever really accepted the principle of cross-
bearing? Do we understand it?

I know one woman who did not! I was her minister. And since that Sunday morning I have had a
deeper conviction that a large part of the preacher's
business is to be a good *teacher*. My sermon theme was

cross-bearing, but as far as that one woman was concerned it could have been anything else.

As she stood before me after the service, she said in all seriousness, "Well, I am trying to bear my cross."

Because I knew her so well I replied, "And what is your cross?"

"Boils!" she answered.

And I knew not whether to laugh or to weep. At length, I said, "Would you like to have me tell you why a boil is not a cross?"

When she nodded I began, "Because my experience is that you can't get rid of boils and you can get rid of the cross." I continued: "I have had fourteen boils myself this spring, and I have tried hard to get rid of them; I can sympathize with you. But a cross is something else; you can get rid of it any time you will. You don't have to carry a cross!"

Shame on us that we should think of associating our little aches and pains with cross-bearing! No, real cross-bearing is doing something that you don't have to do, enduring something that you don't have to endure, and enduring it willingly for love's sake. It was so with Jesus; He didn't have to bear the Cross, but,

> "He saw me plunged in deep distress,
>   He flew to my relief;
> For me He bore the shameful cross,
>   And carried all my grief."

So the question is not, "What is my cross?" but, Do we believe in the *principle of cross-bearing*? To be worth the name cross-bearing must be voluntary. Christians ought never to forget that Jesus, *of His own will,* faced the Cross, and deliberately accepted it as his God-given stewardship.

And Jesus wanted to make this clear. So He says in today's scripture, "I lay down my life. . . . No man taketh it from me. . . . I have power to lay it down." And—thank God—He added, "I have power to take it again."

We must get this point—that *cross-bearing such as Jesus brought into the world must be voluntary!* Do we recall that dark hour following Gethsemane, when Peter slashed around with a sword as the enemy came to take his Lord?

How calm Jesus was at that hour! In spite of all the confusion around Him He told the coming ages two things that will increasingly change the history of the world. One was, "Peter, put up your sword. They that take to the sword will perish with the sword." Today force still remains "The Great Illusion," yet the light is breaking.

But the other truth was still more mighty: "What! do you think I cannot appeal to my Father to furnish me at this moment with over twelve legions of angels?" (Moffatt.) Why didn't He do it?

What He was saying to Peter was: "I don't have to bear the cross, but I am going to. I could wipe out our enemies with force; but force doesn't change anything. Only love conquers! So Jesus accepted the Cross for love's sake. Oh, that every member of Christ's Church might understand His words: "No man taketh my life from me. I lay it down of myself."

* * *

A Prayer

Dear Christ, teach us too the stewardship of the Cross. Teach us the joy of doing the things we ought

to do, and yet the things we will not do except as love,
Thy love, shall lead us on. Help us to be dependable
for Thy name's sake. Amen.

Meditation

"Half the world is on the wrong scent in the pursuit
of happiness. They think it consists in having and
getting and in being served by others. . . . It consists in
giving, and in serving others. He that would be happy,
let him remember that there is but one way—it is more
blessed, it is more happy, to give than to receive."—
Henry Drummond.

At Calvary

Whatever else Thou sendest, oh, send this—
Not ecstasy of love or lover's kiss,
But strength to know the joy of sacrifice,
To see life deeply as with opened eyes!
Oh, grant me this, dear God,
   Through tears or loss—
To know the joyous secret
   Of Thy Cross!

IV

Life Hoarders

"Get behind me, you Satan! You are a hindrance to me!"
(Matthew 16. 23, Moffatt.)

There must have been some strong reason for such
strong language! Our Lord had never called Peter
such a name before—"You Satan!"

Why did Jesus speak thus to His disciple? Only a
short time before (in this same chapter) He had given
Peter great praise, "You are a blessed man, Simon

Bar-jona!" And now so soon, "You Satan!" Why the change?

We recall that shortly after Jesus had praised Peter and had declared that upon his kind of faith "I will build my church," our Lord went on to tell His disciples that the time was approaching when He must go up to Jerusalem "and suffer many things of the elders and chief priests and scribes, and be killed."

At that point the thing happened! Peter took Him and began to reprove Him for what He had said, "God forbid, Lord, this must not be." Then it was that Jesus turned on Peter and said, "Thou Satan!"

But why was Jesus so terribly aroused? He must have been glad for the love that caused His disciples to shrink from the thought of His death. Yes, He was glad for that; but it was not their love that alarmed Him. It was Peter's philosophy of life!

Jesus' words give us the key. He says to Peter, "Your outlook is not God's but man's" (verse 23, Moffatt). It was the old pagan philosophy that Jesus was condemning in such severe terms. This was the philosophy that a good man should not suffer hardships; progress can be made in some other way; cross-bearing is not necessary!

Such philosophy stood squarely in the way of Jesus' teaching that life is a stewardship; it stood squarely in the way of the coming of God's Kingdom. And when Jesus said to Peter, "You Satan! You are a hindrance to me," He was blasting not at the man so much as at his partly pagan creed. Jesus saw that unless the pagan philosophy, that a man's first business is to save his own life and his own interests, could be purged away, then there would be no Christian movement and no godlike personalities on this earth.

The life hoarders are a menace to the Kingdom of God and to themselves! So Jesus warned His disciples in those immortal words, "Whosoever will save his life shall lose it" (Matthew 16. 25). Pity those who would seek the easy Christian life! The laws of the universe are against them. Alfred Russell Wallace gives a wonderful illustration of this in his story of *The Butterfly*. He says: "I came upon the creature beating its wings and struggling wildly to force its way through the narrow neck of the cocoon. I was sorry that so handsome a creature should go through so severe an ordeal. I took out my pocketknife and slit the cocoon. The great moth came out at once, but its glorious colors never developed, its great wings never expanded, its glorious hues and tints never appeared. The moth drooped about and finally died. The furious struggle with the cocoon was the Creator's wise way of developing the wings of the butterfly."

Some years ago the efficient superintendent of one of the departments of our large church school was having home hardships as a result of the business depression. And because it seemed to me that it was unfair for her to carry her added burdens of housework and the heavy task at church, I wrote, offering her some relief. Here is the answer of a real crossbearer:

"And then Wednesday night as I lay awake in bed— those words you used recently, 'I will not render unto the Lord that which cost me nothing,' were like an electric sign before my eyes. I have wished for years that I could do something for my Lord that really cost me something. I've never really done anything hard. I've had such an easy life. I often think that is why

I seemed so abused to myself, at times, and I'm ashamed. I just know that all that we are going through is for some purpose. And then your sermon last Sunday! To use your illustration, can you not see I do not want you to cut my cocoon and let me out easier? I want to fight my own way out! It is costing me something now to keep the department. I intend to keep it!"

* * *

A Prayer

O Thou Lamb of God that taketh away the sin of the world, we need not cry to Thee for mercy; help us to have mercy upon ourselves. Thou hast loved us from the beginning, and Thou wilt forgive us our sins when, despising our repeated weakness, we do, in deed and truth, set our faces to the Cross. Help us, we beseech Thee, for Thy name's sake. Amen.

Meditation

"Do not pray for easy lives! Pray to be stronger men! Do not pray for tasks equal to your powers! Pray for powers equal to your tasks! Then the doing of your work shall be no miracle. But you shall be a miracle. Every day you shall wonder at yourself, at the richness of life which has come in you by the grace of God."—*Phillips Brooks*.

Oh, Let Me Grow

Oh, let me grow!
About me buds are bursting
  And greening trees are yearning toward the sky,
And everywhere is God's good power worsting
  The stagnant earth and lifting life on high.

Oh, let me grow!
Shall I alone be dying
    When earth and sky obey His slightest nod?
Am I a dwarf in God's great universe, defying
    The laws of life that lift men up to God?

Then let me grow!
This world is mere beginning;
    Soul, thou art born for larger things than this;
Eternal mansions wait thy ardent winning,
    Adventures high, the battlements of God, thy
                                    Master's kiss!

V

Presumptuous Sins

"Keep back thy servant also from presumptuous sins"
(Psalms 19. 13).

Another sin against the Cross of Christ is the sin of presumption. The person who commits this type of sin never doubts the goodness and mercies of God, but he fails to appreciate them. He fails to see that the goodness of God is a call to repentance and to action. His is a sin against Jesus' call to stewardship. He just doesn't hear the call. Yet he can sing lustily, "Jesus paid it all, all to Him I owe," but he rests there, presuming on the mercy of God. Sometimes he can even get sentimental about the Cross—even to tears! What this sinner needs is action—some definite acknowledgment and expression of stewardship.

It is this kind of sinner that Saint Paul gets after when he writes, "Despisest thou the riches of his goodness and forbearance and long-suffering; not knowing that the goodness of God leadeth thee to repentance?" (Romans 2. 4.)

I had a dream the other day. I think it was a dream; and yet I seemed awake. An angel stood beside my desk. It was the morning hour. He came as sunlight comes—silently, a warming presence.

I started to arise; but he pushed me back into my chair. The quietness of heaven filled the room. And then I heard him say, half speaking to himself and half to me, "I do not understand!"

"What is it, sir," I said, "that you do not understand?"

"I do not understand these humankind." I waited. He went on:

"Yesterday I saw some children playing where temptations, like black fiends, lay all around. I said if I could only find some Christian soul to spend an hour here, we would do much to save these little ones. And then I looked around for help. And there it came. At least I thought so, for I saw the Emblem on her breast—a gleaming Cross!

" 'Dear sister, God has sent you just in time,' I said. 'Come, spend an hour with these, God's little ones. Come, and while they gather 'round, tell them the wonder stories of the Cross, and guide them at their play! And I, unseen, will help.' "

The angel sighed. "But she would not! She told me of her trivial tasks and hurried on. I watched her as she went, thinking perhaps I was mistaken in the Sign. But no, it hung there right across her breast, a gleaming Cross. Yet carelessly she went away. I do not understand!"

The angel's hand clutched harder at my arm. "That is not all," he said. "Last Lord's Day went I at my task of calling Christians to the house of prayer. It was within a home of comforts that I stood.

" 'Come, it is the hour of worship—the church bells

ring!' So called I to the father of the house—a man sturdy of stature, well within his prime.

"'I did not sleep so very well last night,' he said. 'Let mother and the children go.'

"'You must not yield unto thy lower self,' I cried. 'Come, stir thee up and lead thy children to the house of God!'

"Again the answer, 'No!' Turning away he reached down for the Sunday paper at his side, and hid himself from God—or thought he did! Then as I turned to go I looked again. The Emblem?—was it really there? Yes, there it hung, dangling by a costly chain—the gleaming Cross. Oh, I do not understand!"

The angel paused. "What is it you don't understand?" I asked. "Why should they wear the cross?" he blazed. "It is an ornament to them," I said.

The angel's hand let go my arm. I looked up to his face. It was not pale; it was ghastly white!

"And has it come to this?" he cried. And he was gone.

Was this a dream? I am not sure. At least it was reality! The writer to the Hebrews says, "How shall we escape, if we neglect so great salvation?" (Hebrews 2. 3.)

* * *

A Prayer

O Thou, who didst dedicate in loving stewardship Thy boundless resources for our redemption, receive, we humbly beseech Thee, this our consecration of time and talent, life and possessions, to the glory of Thy holy kingdom, through Jesus Christ, our Lord. Amen.

Meditation

"Do something! No man is born with a mortgage

on his soul; but every man is born a debtor to Time.
Meet this obligation before you find too late that your
life is impoverished and you cannot redeem it."—
Margaret Bird Steinmetz.

Lenten Meditation

I love to come to this still place
    Where deeper peace is always found,
    To kneel as though on holy ground,
And feel my Master face to face.

I do not know how I could live
    If there were not this refuge sweet,
    Where I could linger at His feet
And He to me sweet healing give.

But He will only let me stay
    Until His peace has lifted me
    Up where the dying world I see,
And then He sweetly bids, "Away."

And I have found, if I would keep
    His Presence with me all day through,
    Then I must learn His will to do
And in His harvest fields to reap.

O Christ, Thou Lover of all men,
    Thou unseen Presence ever near,
    Create within me ears to hear,
And grant me eyes that see. Amen.

VI

THE UPLIFTED CHRIST

"And I, if I be lifted up from the earth, will draw all men
unto me" (John 12. 32).

This promise has not been fulfilled! Jesus has not
drawn all men unto Himself. After nineteen hundred
years almost two thirds of the earth's population are
non-Christian, and probably one half of the world's

people have never heard the name of Jesus. Think of it!

I think of it often; but never with any doubt as to the final outcome. I never doubt His statement, "All power is given unto me in heaven and in earth." But I remember that He added the words, "Go ye!"

And we haven't gone! That is the trouble. The Cross is a stewardship, and we have refused to take it up and follow Him. There is no question about the power of Jesus. Every year we see new evidences that His kingdom is coming over the earth. But the coming seems so slow! And it is our fault. We haven't really tried a Christianity with a Cross. There has been such a discrepancy between the Christianity of Jesus and our own! It is not that so many people have never heard of Jesus; the tragic thing is that so many so-called Christians among us show no concern about this.

"Why do you get all 'het up' over the heathen?" said a well-to-do business man to me at the close of my sermon. "Do you think," he continued, "that God is going to send them to hell because they have never heard of Jesus Christ?"

I might have said to him, "No, God isn't going to send them to hell for that reason, but we are going to send ourselves to hell unless we show more concern about those who sit in darkness." Unless we save others we cannot save ourselves!

Just so we are coming to recognize that Jesus put "if" before the prophecy of our scripture, "If I be lifted up." Of course He had in mind the terrible experience of being lifted up by His enemies, but He must also have had it in mind that He must be lifted up by His friends.

Is not this what Paul meant when he said, "I fill up that which is behind in the sufferings of Jesus"? Dr. John Henry Jowett once asked, "Was there anything lacking in the sufferings of Jesus?" And his answer was, "Only one thing—the story needs a teller; the gospel needs a herald, and the gospel of a broken heart demands the ministry of bleeding hearts."

And this is in accord with the philosophy of Jesus that life is a stewardship of love and sacrifice. "I must be about my Father's business," He had said. And when the hour came when the shadow of the cross was very dark, so that He cried, "Now is my soul troubled; and what shall I say? Father, save me from this hour," what He really did say was: "But for this cause came I unto this hour. Father, glorify thy name" (John 12. 27, 28). And then came the triumphant cry, "And I, if I be lifted up from the earth, will draw all men unto me." Why hasn't His joy been accomplished? Why is the world still in such a "troubled mess"? The only possible answer is that the stewardship of Jesus can only be fulfilled by the stewardship of His disciples. Jesus said, "As my Father hath sent me, even so send I you" (John 20. 21). Also He said, "I am the light of the world" (John 8. 12), and then, "Ye are the light of the world" (Matthew 5. 14).

So we conclude that the problem of Christianizing the world is, first of all, the problem of Christianizing the Church. Jesus tried to teach us this, "I pray not for the world, but for them which thou hast given me." Why did He say that? Because He knew that the surest way to save the world was by the way of purified and consecrated souls who would be the faithful stewards of the Cross.

There is a world of significance in the statement of an English bishop, "In the beginning Christianity was kept at a high level by its being dangerous to be a Christian." That was because the early Christians not only gazed up at the Cross in adoration and thanksgiving, but they likewise took up the Cross and followed after their victorious Lord. Strangely enough, they learned that cross-bearing is the greatest joy-bringer in the world.

* * *

A Prayer

O Thou Christ, author and finisher of our faith, who for the joy that was set before Thee endured the Cross, despising the shame, reveal to us this day, we beseech Thee, the secret of Thy power to suffer and endure; and then grant us Thy joy, to the glory of Thy holy name. Amen.

Meditation

"The great, glaring denial of faith and duty which stands out before the world today so clearly that it cannot be concealed, is the refusal of those who bear the name of Christ to execute the great commission which their Master has given them. Christianity is thus made to testify against herself. A thousand Ingersolls in every country under the sun would not do so much to create disbelief of the truth among men as this spectacle of a Church inheriting promises which she seems unable to believe, and receiving commandments which she seems unwilling to execute."—*Bishop James M. Thoburn.*

𝕺𝖇𝖑𝖎𝖛𝖎𝖔𝖓

I

Upon a hill called Calvary
  A Man went forth to die;
He gave His body to a cross—
  They built it huge and high;
They sent Him to oblivion,
  With many a cruel cry!

II

Long years have passed since Calvary;
  Those cruel cries are dead!
Dead too the hands that pressed the thorns
  In torture on His head—
All gone into oblivion;
  He is alive instead!

VII

THE SUPREME INVITATION

"Come, take up the cross, and follow me" (Mark 10. 21).

"Remember that Christianity is not a solitary religion. If you would get to heaven, you must take someone with you." Once upon a time John Wesley heard words like these and he never forgot. Some historians think that a new day began right there in Wesley's experience of God. What do we think about it today? Do we believe the statement, "Christianity is not a solitary religion"? Yes, I think we increasingly believe this; but we don't believe that the supreme appeal of Christianity is, "If you would go to heaven." We have discovered mightier motives, more like the motives that Jesus appealed to. When did He ever say, "Come unto me, and I will take you to heaven"? Yes, He did say, "Come unto me, ... and I will give you rest." But it was rest in the *present* hour

—not merely in some future heaven. Moreover, it wasn't the rest of doing nothing; it was the "rest in the rest of God."

> "Rest is not quitting a busy career,
> Rest is the fitting of self to the sphere."

Let no one suppose that we are questioning the reality of heaven. Oh, no, for those promises concerning the future life are exceeding great and precious. "I go to prepare a place for you. And if I go and prepare a place for you, I will come again, and receive you unto myself" (John 14. 2, 3). Wonderful promise!

We rejoice also in Saint Paul's words, "Henceforth there is laid up for me a crown of righteousness, which the Lord, the righteous judge, shall give me at that day" (2 Timothy 4. 8). But Paul began this triumphant valedictory by saying, "I have fought a good fight, I have finished my course, I have kept the faith." It is evident that in Saint Paul's mind the joys of heaven are the result of keeping "the faith" here on earth. And he learned this from his Lord.

Years ago, in my first year as a parson, a child taught me a lesson that still stings. I met the five-year-old boy on the street one Monday morning. "I missed you at Sunday school yesterday," I said.

"I went with mama and papa to the lake," he answered.

And then the young preacher showed his dumbness. "Well, you ought to go to church first. Don't you want to learn about Jesus, and get ready to go to heaven when you die?"

Whereupon the youngster came back with these words, "I ain't never goin' to die." Of course he wasn't!

No, the call of Christ was not primarily a call to go to heaven; it was a call to get right with life and with God. It was a call to battle—a call to bear a cross in a great cause. To the young man whose life was being made flabby and soft by luxuries and ease, He said, "Come, take up the cross, and follow me." But he "went away sorrowful." The cross was too much for him. He couldn't take it! He wanted something easy. And how much he missed!

> O the sheer joy of it, living with Thee,
> God of the universe, Lord of a tree,
> Maker of mountains, lover of me!

One of the most heart-moving pictures in the New Testament is that of the Master as He watches the young rich man turn sorrowfully away. How Jesus loved him and longed for his life in the Kingdom! There is great passion stored up in those first words which He spoke to His watching disciples as He turned away from the departing youth and said, "How difficult it is for those who have money to get into the Realm of God!" It must be that money is more dangerous than we know. And yet there are other gods that lure men from the Lord of Life.

* * *

A Prayer

O Lord, turn Thy light upon any unconsecrated corner of my heart. Help me to know myself. Too readily am I able to see the faults of others; show me mine own. Search Thou my heart; discover to me the hidden idols; help me to tear them down; O Thou blessed Redeemer, "break down every idol throne, reign supreme and reign alone." Amen.

Meditation

"Ten Christians that become notably different and far better Christians would produce a greater effect in the world than a hundred who were induced to enter the Christian life for the first time.... The world will begin to wonder at the Church far more through something that happens to the Christian people themselves than it will through some showy and dramatic increase of its numbers."—*Henry Drummond*.

Busy Inns

Let not our hearts be busy inns
 That have no room for Thee,
But cradles for the living Christ
 And His Nativity.

Still driven by a thousand cares
 The pilgrims come and go;
The hurried caravans press on,
 The inns are crowded so!

No room for little helpless hands,
 For mothers' cries no place;
The great of every land are here,
 No room for baby's face!

Here are the rich and busy ones,
 With things that must be sold,
No room for simple things within
 This hostelry of gold.

Yet hunger dwells within these walls,
 These shining walls and bright,
And blindness groping here and there
 Without a ray of light.

Oh, lest we starve or lest we die
 In our stupidity,
O come, Thou Child, within and share
 Our hospitality.

Let not our hearts be busy inns
 That have no room for Thee,
But cradles for the living Christ
 And His Nativity.

CHAPTER FIVE

𝕳𝖔𝖓𝖊𝖘𝖙 𝕬𝖈𝖐𝖓𝖔𝖜𝖑𝖊𝖉𝖌𝖒𝖊𝖓𝖙

I

A HOLY REMINDER

"Thou shalt not eat of it" (Genesis 2. 17).

THERE is a paragraph in the ritual of various churches which affirms that "God's sovereign ownership and man's stewardship ought to be acknowledged" in certain definite ways. Why?

For the same reason that an honest churchman recently gave when he said, "I'm through with lying in my hymn-singing!" Then he added, "I am not going to sing anything hereafter that I don't really mean. A Christian ought to be honest to say the least."

Well, that is one reason why we need some kind of concrete method of making acknowledgment of God's ownership and of our stewardship. To say the least, we ought to be honest in our religion. This is why Jesus declared at the close of the Sermon on the Mount, "Not every one that saith unto me, Lord, Lord, shall enter into the kingdom of heaven; but he that doeth the will of my Father" (Matthew 7. 21). It is terribly easy to become a hypocrite!

I think God saw the need of such acknowledgment in the beginning. Whatever else the forbidden tree in the garden of Eden signifies, it certainly stands as a reminder to Adam and his partner (and to all the rest of us!) that the garden belonged to the Creator

111

and they were only the caretakers, the "guests of God." The beautiful story runs like this: "The Lord God took the man, and put him into the garden of Eden to dress it and to keep it" (Genesis 2. 15). He could partake freely of everything in the garden except one tree which was holy unto the Lord! "Thou shalt not eat of it," was the order. Everybody really needs something like that to keep him in his place, to remind him that God is really the owner, and he is only the caretaker.

Out in California a great redwood tree towers up into the heavens. The lofty majesty of it makes one think of the God who, through centuries, has fed it and loved it. One feels like kneeling beneath it. There it stands to the glory of the Almighty. And yet some persons, lacking both in reverence and humor, have put a bronze tablet on it with these words, "Dedicated to the memory of ———."

When does the Creator give up His title to His creation? The answer is, Never! That noble tree and the ridiculous bronze tablet are a warning: How easy it is for man to appropriate for himself what belongs to God! "The silver and gold are mine," said the Lord; but the man of business finds it difficult to think of tangible things, like gold and oil and trees, as belonging to an intangible and invisible Presence.

This is why we need some method of regularly and honestly acknowledging God's ownership if we are truly to be stewards of life and time and all. When the Two Companions of Eden appropriated for themselves "the holy portion," which was sacred to God alone, were they not really destroying the signboard which God had posted in the garden? Was not this the way it read?—"This tree is holy unto the Lord.

It is your reminder that this is God's garden and you
are God's partners. Touch it not."

Now, this is not a merely academic consideration.
It is a very practical matter. It is no easy thing for one
to bring the idea of God's ownership of all things into
the realm of the real; but it is a very important thing.
For example, it is no mere ornamental feature of our
worship that we stand to sing

"All things come of Thee, O Lord,
    And of Thine own have we given Thee."

True, this does add to the worshipfulness of the
service, but there is an important educational element
here. We have been worshiping with "our tithes and
offerings." It ought not to have been merely "taking
a collection." It was worship! It was a holy acknowledgment that our Heavenly Father is the Giver of all
that we have. God help us if we were lying when we
sang those words!

Just so, it is most important that we keep some
"forbidden trees" in the garden of our lives that are
holy unto the Lord! Evidently, we need such holy
habits of worship if we are to lift God and His gifts out
of the abstract into reality.

* * *

A Prayer

O God, help us to make Thee real this day. Help
us to make Thee real at any cost. Help us to realize
that we can make Thee real if we are ready to heed
the guideposts Thou hast set up along the way. O
may we live as in the Garden of the Lord this day.
In Christ's dear name. Amen.

Meditation

"How difficult it is for the businessman to live unselfishly! He must bear the handicap of a life whose
main purpose is the accumulation of money. . . . But
who is the most successful businessman? Not neces-
sarily the man who has the largest bank account; that
is one measure of success, but not the truest. The most
successful businessman is he who renders the greatest
service to mankind, and whose life is most useful."—
William E. Sweet.

Among the Redwoods

I heard God speak today,
I heard Him speak majestically;
From out the Redwood's height,
In grand high tone,
He spoke!
The world grew hushed,
We stood alone!
Then did I hear Him
Speak the psalmist's lay:
"Be still, for I am God"—
This did He say!

II

THE LOYALTY TEST

"Whosoever doth not bear his cross, and come after me,
cannot be my disciple" (Luke 14. 27).

"Jimmy, will you give some of your blood to save
your sister's life?"

The surgeon asked the question of a strapping boy
just about to enter his teens. But he didn't get any
answer. Jimmy was thinking hard and at the same
time trying to get rid of the lump in his throat.

Jimmy's sister was very sick and the doctors had

agreed that only a transfusion could save her life.
They had first tested her father's blood. It wouldn't
do. Then mother's and the older sister's were checked
in vain. Then came Jimmy's turn and the test was
satisfactory. Poor Jimmy!

Again the doctor's question and Jimmy's struggle.
He saw himself bleeding to death. He even caught a
glimpse of the graveyard! But his sister needed his
blood and he was thinking hard. What should a real
brother do?

For the third time the surgeon asked, "Jimmy, do
you hear? Will you give your blood to save your
sister's life?"

So Jimmy clenched his fists, looked the doctor in
the face, and snapped, "Yes, sir!" A few minutes later,
in the operating room by the side of his sister, they
were pumping his fine healthy blood into the veins
of a very sick girl. Nobody seemed much concerned
about him, he thought. Finally the doctor noticed
the pallor of his face. "Do you feel sick, Jimmy?"
But the teeth only went harder shut. Then silence.
Then the boy whispered, "Doctor!"

"What is it, Jimmy?"

With tightly closed eyes, "Say, Doctor, how long
will it be before I die?"

Laugh? Of course we may, but it was no laughing
matter to Jimmy.

I have thought of this newspaper story many times.
And I always end by picturing that evening-time when
the lad was lovingly tucked in bed by his happy mother
and he himself *the happiest boy in town!*

The author of one of the New Testament books, in
a noble reference to Jesus, says, "Who for the joy that
was set before him endured the cross" (Hebrews 12.

2). As for Jimmy there had been no visions of "joy" in connection with his cross-bearing. But nevertheless he had met the test; and the "joy" had come. It is always so! One thing was clear, Jimmy's loyalty to his sister was no mere profession. He had made the honest acknowledgment expected of a brother who professes to love his sister. It is this honest proof of loyalty that our Lord appears to expect in today's scripture. He says, "Whosoever doth not bear his cross, and come after me, cannot be my disciple." Any other kind of disciple is just a poor imitation of the real thing.

We have laughed at many illustrations to the contrary, but they are always tragic. For instance, only yesterday some laymen repeated to me the old story of the minister at the funeral, who, looking into the casket, said, "This corpse has been a member of this church for thirty years." We may laugh at these stories, but they have tragedy behind them.

In today's parable Jesus makes clear why He can do nothing with the indifferent disciple. Picture the background of this story: Jesus is walking to His next appointment, "and there went great multitudes with him." The scripture says that He turned and said something unto them. What was it, and why? Any pastor who has meditated over his church membership records can understand the meditation of Jesus. "How could He ever build a Kingdom with this half-hearted kind of followers?" Then He turned and faced them. And in the hush He shocked them with His words about the cross.

"You cannot be a disciple of mine," He said, "not until you are ready, for the sake of the Cause, to put your very lives upon a cross."

Then He told them about the Cause He had come

to lead. First, He pictures Himself as the Builder, "Which man of you, if you had a tower to build, would not study to see if you had the stuff with which to build it?"

Then He pictures Himself as the King, and says, "What king sets out to fight" without deliberating whether his soldiers are of such heroic caliber that with ten thousand he can dare to go against twice the number? Read that stirring challenge.

Well, there is much more to this parable, but all in all it is a monumental advertisement that the call of Christ is a call to holy war, a call to enlist in the Kingdom-Cause!

> "While kings of eternal evil
>   Yet darken the hills about,
> Thy part is with broken saber
>   To rise on the last redoubt;
> To fear not sensible failure,
>   Nor covet the game at all,
> But, fighting, fighting, fighting,
>   Die, driven against the wall."
>   —*Louise Imogen Guiney.*

* * *

A Prayer

Blessed Christ, who hast taught us that we may have life and have it more abundantly, purify our vision, we beseech Thee, that being enabled to see Thee as the enlarger of all life, we may perfectly abandon ourselves to Thy holy will, and find in Thee our largest consummation and bliss. Amen.

Meditation

"It is not so much resolution as renunciation, not so much courage as resignation, that we need. He that has once yielded to God will yield to nothing but God."—*John Ruskin*.

My Faith

I want the faith
That envies not
The passing of the days;
That sees all times and ways
More endless than the stars;
That looks at life,
Not as a little day
Of heat and strife,
But one eternal revel of delight
With God, the friend, adventurer, and light.
What matter if one chapter nears the end?
What matter if the silver deck the brow?
Chanting I go
Past crimson flaming
From the autumn hills,
Past winter's snow,
To find that glad new chapter
Where God's spring
Shall lift its everlasting voice to sing.
This is the faith I seek;
It shall be mine,
A faith that strides across the peaks of time!

III

STEALING THE VINEYARD

"What therefore shall the lord of the vineyard do unto them?" (Luke 20. 15.)

One of the best known of Jesus' stewardship parables is this of the vineyard. It must be remembered that the wicked husbandmen were churchmen; and their fundamental wickedness lay in their refusal to give an honest acknowledgment to the owner of the vineyard. It was the story over again of the forbidden fruit and the garden.

"In vain we call old notions fudge,
    And bend our conscience to our dealing,
The Ten Commandments will not budge.
    And stealing will continue stealing."

But probably those husbandmen would have said: "We didn't intend to steal. The Owner had been gone so long and seemed so far away! Moreover, we ourselves had put a good deal into that vineyard; so we came to think of it as our very own." Here is an illustration from a current magazine as to how easy such reasoning is:

"Why, my old dad built this business from the ground up; built it with his keen Yankee brain, and in doing that he gave this town the biggest shove it ever had. He always paid good wages, and he looked out for his men, but he knew who *owned* the shop, you bet, and who ran it! He hadn't any partner until he took me in; and when Tom undertakes to tell me that I have got any partners outside of himself, I figure it is up to me to prove that he is mistaken—even if I have to show him that I haven't any partners at all." Thus have men at all times forgotten God's ownership of the vineyard!

The lesson of this parable is perfectly plain: "A certain man planted a vineyard, and let it forth to husbandmen, and went into a far country for a long time" (Luke 20. 9). Probably the owner was not as far away as they thought. God always seems "far away" to the rebellious and disobedient. But to those who reverence and obey Him He becomes nearer and nearer. At least the owner was near enough to send for an honest acknowledgment of his ownership. "And at the season he sent a servant to the husbandmen, that they should give him of the fruit of the vineyard; but the husbandmen beat him, and sent him away empty" (verse 10). Two more times this was repeated, with the same results. The faithless stewards treated the messengers shamefully and sent them away empty. Then patiently and with great yearning the owner made one supreme appeal: "Then said the lord of the vineyard, What shall I do? I will send my beloved son: it may be that they will reverence him" (verse 13). But they didn't reverence him. They killed him.

Thus Jesus, in His parable of the vineyard, connects His approaching death with the dishonest stewardship of the leaders of religion. Leadership is always a serious responsibility, but leadership in religious things is most serious of all. It may be used mightily for the building of the Kingdom, or it may be betrayed in terrible selfishness. Neither a nation nor a church can rise higher than its leaders, and it is a question whether they should.

When Jesus asked, "What will the owner of the vineyard do to these killers of his son?" and answered the question by saying, "He shall come and destroy these husbandmen, and shall give the vineyard to others," the people shuddered and said, "God forbid!" And the "chief priests and the scribes sought to lay hands on him; . . . for they perceived that he had spoken this parable against them" (Luke 20. 19).

But neither the pious phrases of the people, nor the revengeful spirit of the dictators, could suffice to avert catastrophe. Always there must be repentance and a return to God on the part of the leaders and the led. Nearly two thousand years have passed since they cast the "beloved Son" out of the vineyard, but the story is not yet done.

A Prayer

Have mercy upon us, O God, according to Thy tender mercies. Forgive us that so often in our selfishness we forget Thy kingdom. The cares of the office and the home press heavily upon us and we crowd Thee out of Thy vineyard. Forgive us, Lord, and give us grace to try again. In Jesus' name. Amen.

Meditation

Creation was a supreme venture on the part of God in producing a breed of men who would share with Him the enjoyment and administration of His boundless resources. No yearning mother could bend more wistfully over the cradle of her child than did God over the cradle of the race. Only a parent who has knelt beside some little cot to pray that his first born might be a blessing to the world, can know how eagerly God planned that garden "to grow every tree that is pleasant," and how yearningly He desired that the child should share his Father's passion for the welfare of the world.

Christmas Message

What is the message the heavens are telling?
   What is this song from the place of His birth?
Hear it, O hear it, the sweet strains are swelling;
   What is this music that sweeps o'er the earth?

Shepherd, come tell me, what was that sweet message,
   Born from the skies to your hungering heart?
I too am hungry for something I know not—
   Whisper it softly, the tidings impart.

And O ye kings, come tell me your secret,
   Why did you journey in hope from afar?
What was the hunger within your hearts burning;
   Why did you yearningly follow the star?

Ah, well! I know what the heavens are telling,
　Ah, well! I know what your answer would be,
Shepherd or king, from the mansion or cottage,
　All the world shares in that longing with thee:

"O that I knew Him"—the cry of the ages!
　"O that I knew One in heaven who shares
All of earth's sorrows, its joys, and its heartaches,
　O that I knew of a Father who cares!"

Then came the music! O heavens, keep telling!
　Sing in my heart thy sweet story of love;
Jesus, Redeemer, best gift of the Father,
　Give us the Christmas that's born from above!

IV

THE LEAKS OF LIFE

"That ye might be filled with all the fullness of God"
(Ephesians 3. 19).

From the parable of the vineyard we may suppose
that one of the most shameful things that the angels
look down upon is the reluctance of professing Christians to give of their time, talents, and possessions to
the support of the Kingdom. How often, with our
petty schemes of raising money for the church, the
Lord of the whole earth is made to appear as a beggar
in His own vineyard! But the worst of it is that stinginess and greed reap their own harvests in moral and
spiritual suicide. It is the story of the Dead Sea over
again:

> "All tributary streams
> 　Found here their grave,
> Because that sea received
> 　But never gave!"

The dwarfed and shriveled soul is what grieves God
most, that Christ should have died in vain, that the
stealing of the vineyard should still go on.

The tragedy is not merely that the Church is halted in its mission of salvation for lack of the gifts of money and prayer and other things. No, the tragedy is that so many professing Christians do not give away enough of themselves to keep what is left of themselves vital and glad. "These things have I spoken unto you," Jesus said, "that my joy might remain in you, and that your joy might be full" (John 15. 11).

And this was just what Saint Paul prayed for the Ephesian Christians: "For this cause I bow my knees unto the Father of our Lord Jesus Christ . . . that he would grant you . . . to be strengthened with might by his Spirit in the inner man; . . . that *ye might be filled with all the fullness of God*" (Ephesians 3. 14, 16, 19).

Now, the theme of today's study is just this: How are we to be *"filled* with all the fullness of God"? The filling is, of course, the work of the Holy Spirit, but the emptying and the making a prepared place for Him is our own work. There ought to be no mystery or magic about the whole operation. It means, first of all, honest co-operation between the professed disciple and the Spirit of the Lord.

The other day I found in an old notebook a significant sentence. It has quotation marks around it. Referring to the work of the Holy Spirit, the speaker said, "What we first need is not filling, but soldering." The thought is, of course, that every man has leaks which he himself is expected to take care of before he can ask the Holy Spirit to fill the temple.

It was a similar illustration that a distinguished English preacher gave me last summer. He said that in one of the suburban churches of London there was a layman who was forever repeating, in a weekly prayer service, his petition to be "filled with the Spirit." The prayer was evidently a hang-over from more vital days, for the member's life never seemed to give evidence that his prayer was answered.

There was at least one man who thought he knew the reason. And one night as the brother was saying his customary prayer, "Lord, fill me: fill me, Lord!" the deacon was heard to ejaculate, "Lord, it's no use; he leaks!"

Judged from Scripture and experience, the deacon was right in his theory. No one can hope to know the Spirit-filled life without giving honest attention to "the leaks."

> Breathe on us, Holy Spirit,
>   Not with the tempest din,
> But as the breath of heaven
>   Come, purify within.
>
> Burn in us, Holy Spirit,
>   Burn as a tongue of fire
> Invisibly within our hearts,
>   Burn out each base desire.

* * *

A Prayer

Dear Christ, for this cause we also bow our knees to the Father, that we may be filled with all the fullness of God. It is love, joy, peace, power—these are the things most needed by the world. But Thou hast called us to the channels of Thy grace. Without Thee we can do nothing, but without us the Kingdom halts. O Thou Searcher of hearts, show us wherein we can make advance with Thee this day. And Thine be the glory. Amen.

Meditation

"All experience comes to be but more and more of pressure of His life on ours. I cannot tell you how personal this grows to me—He is here—and I know Him. It is no figure of speech. It is the realest thing in the world, and every day makes it more real, and one wonders with delight what it will grow to as the years go on."—*Phillips Brooks*.

The Host

Hearken, brothers, do you hear it?
"Ye are temples of the Spirit!"
Hearken, then, oh, give it credit,
He, the Lord of Heaven, said it.

Hearken, brothers, do you hear it?
You are Stewards of the Spirit,
And your brain and heart and hands,
He, the Holy Ghost, commands.

Not as guest, but as the Host,
Comes this blessed Holy Ghost;
If I let Him have His way,
He will come and He will stay.

Dear Lord, not in our guest chamber;
Come and take the whole remainder,
Every room, Lord—I am willing—
Shall possess Thy glad infilling!

V

REDEEMING THE TIME

"Make the very most of your time" (Colossians 4. 5, Moffatt).

Can a loafer and a Christian live in the same body? In answering this question it must be remembered that physical loafing is not the only loafing which threatens a soul's welfare. There are mental loafers—and spiritual loafers too. Saint Paul's appeal to the Colossian Christians to "make the very most of your time" is forever a timely appeal. "I must work the works of him that sent me while it is day," said Jesus, "the night cometh." And said the psalmist, "We spend our years as a tale that is told." How quickly they are gone!

> "Time, like an ever rolling stream,
>   Bears all its sons away;
> They fly, forgotten, as a dream
>   Dies at the opening day."

Recently a dying millionaire exclaimed, "I have piles of money, but what good does it do me now?" Yes, what a waste of years, just piling up money! Again the psalmist prays, "So teach us to number our days, that we may apply our hearts unto wisdom."

As regards carelessness there are three things that most generally take the keenness from the life of professing Christians, namely, carelessness with time, carelessness with prayer, and carelessness with money. Very often these three sorry sisters live together, and, sooner or later, it is a gloomy house. Carelessness with time is the central theme of the parable of the ten virgins (Matthew 25. 1-13). There is no more vivid picture of stupid stewardship to be found in the Scriptures. The "stupid virgins" are so stupid that we have to remind ourselves that it is Jesus who is telling this story, for it doesn't seem possible that any five persons could be as stupid as these. Think of carrying around lamps without oil! But it may be that Jesus is saying to us in parable this very thing: That five out of every ten members of our churches are just as stupid as this. For it is certainly true, in most churches, that at least one half of the people let the other half pay the bills, carry the responsibilities, and burn the oil.

But note that the great Teacher isn't wasting **any** pity on those who carry the load! Burden-bearing **does** something to us; it makes us strong and confident when the crises come. So when the cry went up, "Here is the bridegroom!" the dependable people went into the marriage feast. It is always so.

Dare we ask the other question that suggests itself? Will half of the members of our group—that great body of indifferent church members—be excluded finally by the Bridegroom? Is this to be the outcome of negligence toward the Church and the Kingdom—of failure in the stewardship of time? For answer we dare not say more than to quote the bridegroom's word to the stupid virgins, "I tell you frankly I do not know you." "And the door was shut." But one thing seems sure in this regard; the closed door is not the result of the arbitrary will of the Bridegroom. Is it not that the "stupid virgins" have never really given time to prepare themselves for the Great Day? The athlete must train for the coming race. The musician must practice scales. The scholar must apply himself. Can anyone suppose that spiritual life and power can just happen? Spiritual deadness and illiteracy are the result of the inexcusable misuse of time. The closed door is the consequence of our own doings!

Suppose we modernize the story. Listen to one of the wise virgins. She is ready to start out for the rendezvous. Her lamp is full of oil. "Oh, I suppose," she is saying, "that I ought to call that careless little friend of mine and warn her to fill her lamp."

And the other girl: "Oh, dear, I forgot to get oil. I'm always in such a hurry. I do wish I could get caught up on things."

Whereupon her mother exclaims: "You could if you would get up in the morning! Yes, and go to bed when you ought."

And then "the stupid virgin" dismisses her worries with, "Oh, well, I can borrow some oil from Mary. She's such a lovely lady."

But it is not youth only that talks the language of the careless, for the habits of youth cling to us across the years, and in age they curse us! So Saint Paul urges, "Make the very most of your time!"

* * *

A Prayer

O Lord, how I love Thy law! Surely, it is better to be a doorkeeper in the house of my God than to possess the riches of the world for a season. Hold me steadily in Thy presence; let not the vain ambitions of this world enthrall me. Be Thou my strength; give me Thy joy, that, always master of the world, it may never master me. Through Jesus Christ, my Lord. Amen.

Meditation

"It took forty years to season Moses so that he was sufficiently prepared to lead the people of God out of the bondage of Egypt in the Land of Promise. The Exodus did not make him; it only proved that he was ready for an emergency by knowing the source and surety of his reserve spiritual forces. ... As the lighted lamp was the passport to the banquet of the bridegroom and the bride, *so spiritual preparedness is the passport to life's greatest conquests.* Crises never grow character, they only reveal it."—*Roswell C. Long.*

I Will Not Hurry

I will not hurry through this day!
Lord, I will listen by the way,
To humming bees and singing birds,
To murmuring trees and friendly words;
And for the moments in between
Seek glimpses of Thy great Unseen.

I will not hurry through this day,
I will take time to think and pray;
I will look up into the sky,
Where fleecy clouds and swallows fly;
And somewhere in the day, maybe
I will catch whispers, Lord, from Thee!

VI

The Sabbath Acknowledgment

"Remember the sabbath day, to keep it holy" (Exodus 20. 8).

Yesterday's parable of the ten virgins compels an important question. It is this: How are we going to safeguard ourselves against this peril of the careless use of time? It would seem true, first of all, that there must be an awakening to the fact that the greatest task anyone faces in this life is the building of a personality that can meet the crises of life without being wrecked. "The winds blew and beat upon that house, and it fell: *and great was the fall of it*" (Matthew 7. 27). This is Jesus' first warning.

In the second place, this building of an imperishable personality demands the wise use of the days of the year, together with the hours of the days. "So teach us to number our days, that we may apply our hearts unto wisdom" (Psalm 90. 12). Evidently, the psalmist was an advocate of "the budgeting of time." One of the most impressive prayers in the *Hymnal* is

that which we most frequently sing at the New Year's
season:

> "Another year is dawning,
>   Dear Master, let it be,
> In working or in waiting,
>   Another year with Thee."

But no one knew better than Frances R. Havergal,
the author of these lines, that such a prayer could be
answered only as the one who prayed it should plan
his time schedule in such a way that, morning, noon,
and night, God would have a chance with him. How
can anyone who carelessly starts out in the morning,
with no greeting to God and with no request for
guidance, expect to enjoy even the slightest sense of
companionship with God?

Dr. Roswell C. Long, in an excellent chapter on
"The Stewardship of Time,"[1] quotes "Bordon of
Yale," who died in Egypt on his way to the foreign-
mission field, leaving behind more than a million dollars to continue his work as a steward of Christ. While
a sophomore at Yale the young Christian wrote the
following very suggestive lines in his diary: "I figured
up yesterday where my time went per week and found
that thirty-five hours are wasted somehow. I am
going to see if I can't systematize it so as to get the
most out of them."

This whole matter of the budgeting of time is of
far greater importance than is indicated by the space
we are here able to give to it. But in this day's discussion I desire to face one supreme consideration: The
first item to be set down in any effective budgeting of
time ought to be the ancient command, "Remember

---

[1] *Stewardship Parables of Jesus*, p. 110. Used by permission of Cokesbury Press.

the Sabbath day, to keep it holy." For men and nations there is no more fundamental beginning of a time budget.

But why keep one day holy? Why not keep all the days holy? Surely, not because the sun shines differently, or because the skies are bluer, or because there is any magic in the air on the Sabbath! It seems to me that, fundamental to all other reasons, God set apart the Sabbath day in order that we might have a concrete way of honestly acknowledging that all the days are His days. The peril that threatens us from the present widespread carelessness concerning the Lord's day is not merely that the day itself is being so widely profaned, but also that when we cease to give God a special chance with us on one day, we find ourselves shutting Him out of all of our days.

And when Jesus said, "The sabbath was made for man, and not man for the sabbath" (Mark 2. 27), He had in mind that a man has more than a physical body to be exercised; man has a mind to improve and an eternal soul to save.

But here is someone saying, "We need have no fear about the Sabbath day if we will drive home to every Christian the neglected truth that God owns every day." But is not this like saying that one doesn't need to learn the A B C's if one will learn the alphabet? It is true—profoundly true—that God owns every day. But we begin to realize this only *after* we have first acknowledged that God owns one of the days. Let us really "sanctify the Sabbath" and there is some chance that we may come to sanctify all the days. And so the Lord's Day becomes for the Christian a day of testing and a day of acknowledgment!

A Prayer

Dear Christ, Thou didst say, "I am the light of the world;" and then to Thy disciples, "Ye are the light of the world." O help us, that we may let our lights so shine before men that they may take knowledge of Thee, our Living Lord. Amen.

Meditation

"Dean de Labilliere reminds us that *when Voltaire was asked, 'How would you get rid of this Christian religion?' he replied, 'All you have to do is to abolish Sunday.'* And the Dean suggests why Voltaire was right: 'If the secularizing of Sunday means, as it does mean, that the young people of our land do not learn in their formative years the principles of Christ for common life, then the whole religious and social welfare of the future is endangered.' "—*Federal Council Bulletin.*

Too Busy

"I'm busy!
　No, I cannot stay,
　A thousand things
　　Call me away;
Tomorrow
　I will stop to pray."
And so I lost me
　One great day!

"I'm busy!
　Yes, so I must wait,
　A thousand things
　　Without my gate
Warn that tomorrow
　Is too late
To pray."
And so I saved me
　One great day!

VII

HOLY HABITS

"As his custom was, he went into the synagogue on the sabbath day" (Luke 4. 16).

Evidently it was a holy habit with Jesus to "go to worship" on the Sabbath. And He had other holy habits. For instance, "In the morning, . . . he rose up and went out, and departed into a desert place, and there prayed" (Mark 1. 35). If Jesus needed these holy habits, we may be sure that we do.

So I profoundly believe in holy habits, and I believe that a mighty church-wide insistence upon them is necessary before we can heal our backslidings. I am thinking of holy habits as related to prayer, to church attendance, to Sunday observance, to Bible reading and family worship, and to the proportionate giving of our money. A good habit keeps you going when your moral and spiritual engine gets stalled. Moreover, the habit will start the engine again—just as happens with your automobile. It is my conviction that one layman who has learned to put his life under the yoke of holy habits is worth at least a hundred of the "spasm" variety.

What do we mean by the "spasm" variety? Years ago, on a bright spring morning, I got answer to this question. It happened this way: As I walked across my garden the spring breezes blew a mighty good story to my very feet. I picked up the stray sheet from a religious journal, and had my attention fixed on one section of a serial story, "The Conversion of Miss Cynthia." It was a very interesting account of this maiden woman, who, after a conversion late in life, enthusiastically starts out, at the request of her pastor, to invite the neighborhood to the "revival meetings." She came at length to a home where the ringing of the front doorbell failed to arouse any response. So she went around to the back door and ran full into the lady of the house—mopping her kitchen! Naturally, her welcome was not very cordial, but Miss Cynthia got in. She sat quietly, with her feet safely raised on the rounds of the kitchen chair—safe from the mop— waiting for her hostess to sweeten up.

Then came the wonderful transformation. It happened thus: Miss Cynthia had arrived at the moment when she dared to say, "I came to invite you to the revival meetings at our church." Then, according to my scrap of the story, the strange thing happened. The mop dropped. The woman sat down. A new expression came over her face, as she said: "Revivals! You don't say! Why, I'm so glad to hear it. Yes, indeed, we'll come. *Why John and me have got religion every winter at revivals for the last twenty years!*"

And then it was Miss Cynthia's turn. Being new in church matters, she was puzzled. "What did you say? That you got religion every winter for how many years? I don't understand. How could that be: what did you do with your religion from one winter to another?"

But the lady of the mop was not to be bothered by so insignificant a question, "O laws, I don't know. I never thought of that. But somehow when summer comes it just seems to peter out."

Let it be understood that I am not using this illllustration, blown to me on the spring breezes so many years ago, to cast any reflection upon special meetings for the revival of church people. I presume we must deal with human nature as it is. As long as there are revivals in politics and revivals in business and many other kinds of revivals, we will need revivals in religion. In my own pastorates I do not remember a single church year when I have not made profitable efforts to revive my people and the surrounding neighborhood.

Yes, we need revivals. But the tragedy is that so many need to be revived *who ought to know how to revive themselves, and to keep revived!* Somehow we ought to be able to carry out a program of religious education that would graduate—or elevate—more of our people to the place where they would think less of religion in terms of "spasms" and more in terms of holy habits.

* * *

A Prayer

Dear Christ, help me this day to keep the holy habits Thou didst teach. I know how much I need them in the barren hours when God seems so far away and life so empty. But help me never to mistake, to think of holy habits as the end, for I need Thee, not habits, but Thyself, dear Lord. Amen.

Meditation

"There cannot be a spiritual church, a forward-looking church, a church truly prospering unless minister and members feed daily upon the Word of God, meet God daily in the place of prayer, cling loyally to the church, and walk with Christ 'in lowly paths of service free.' Somehow we have got to get these simple, character-building, spirituality-producing habits back into the lives of our people. It will not be an easy thing to do, but it will have to be done if we are to have a spiritual revival, a reclothing of the Church with the power of God."—*W. E. McCulloch, in Federal Council Bulletin.*

The Prize

Not fame
Nor earthly recompense
I ask, just holy sense
With each returning day,
And grace enough to see and seize
The joy that comes
A-breathing on the breeze,
The joy that comes
A-shining from the trees!

Grant me the grace,
The set of face,
To grow where I have grown,
To know what I have known,
To look not far away
To some tomorrow day
For roses and greensward;
Life brings its own reward
Today, and earth's applaud
Dies out in comradeship with God!

CHAPTER SIX

The Prayer-Stewards

I

THE FIRST WORK

"I exhort therefore, that, first of all, supplications, prayers, intercessions, and giving of thanks, be made for all men" (1 Timothy 2. 1).

THE stewards of prayer! Who are they? Well, they are not too numerous. But here and there in the Old Testament, and, in increasing numbers, in the New Testament and in the present hour, are these spiritual pioneers, these frontiersmen of the Spirit, who go even beyond Alfred Tennyson in discerning that

> "More things are wrought by prayer
> Than this world dreams of."

The prayer-steward not only realizes that intercession is indispensable to his own fellowship with Christ, but he has learned also that without prayer—a regular, insistent, continuous program of prayer—little can be accomplished in building the kingdom of God in the earth.

The prayer-steward has discovered that, for some reason, our Father in heaven has found it wise to make truly surrendered souls partners with Him in releasing the spiritual resources of God. On what other theory can we account for Samuel crying, "God forbid that I should sin against the Lord in ceasing to pray for you"? (1 Samuel 12. 23.) Or a Saint Paul exhorting

137

his people to make prayer their first business? "I exhort therefore, that, first of all, . . . intercessions . . . be made for all men" (1 Timothy 2. 1). Or why should Jesus say to His disciples, "The harvest truly is plenteous, but the laborers are few; pray ye therefore the Lord of the harvest, that he will send forth laborers into his harvest"? (Matthew 9. 37, 38.) Why should I ask the Lord to send forth laborers into the harvest fields unless He has appointed me a steward of this world redemption business?

> "O Thou, by whom we come to God,
>   The Life, the Truth, the Way;
> The path of prayer Thyself hast trod:
>   Lord, teach us how to pray!"

When all the Kingdom victories are finally accounted for, wouldn't it be startling if it should be discovered that the most important work that the Kingdom-men have accomplished in any age has been the work of praying?

It would be startling, but it would not be strange! For, if we could only believe, this is what the Scriptures promise. Prayer is the first work! Before one can accomplish anything for the Kingdom one must learn to pray. As someone has said, "You can do more than pray *after* you have prayed, but you cannot do more than pray until you have prayed."

Similar words came not long since from one of America's most outstanding ministers: "If I could live my life over again," he said, "I would have one thing different. I do not feel that I would put any more time into my study or upon my sermons; nor would I give more attention than I have to my pastoral labors; but I would give infinitely more time to prayer. Here is where I have failed."

So have many others of us failed at this point. Probably the reason is that we haven't realized as we should that prayer is our first work. If it is true, as an American layman recently wrote, that "religion is still in the stagecoach period," then our backwardness can first be located in our failure to practice prayer as Jesus commanded.

Perhaps none will ever understand fully the stewardship of prayer until he sees needs such as Jesus saw and feels a compassion such as He felt. It was then that Jesus said to His disciples, "The harvest truly is plenteous, but the laborers are few; pray ye therefore the Lord of the harvest."

Truly, prayer is our first work and the mightiest we can do. Some years ago Dr. Robert E. Speer wrote, "If fifty men of our generation will enter the holy place of prayer, and become henceforth men whose hearts God has touched with the prayer passion, the history of the Church will be changed."

* * *

A Prayer

"O Thou, who camest from above,
    The pure celestial fire to impart,
Kindle a flame of sacred love
    On the mean altar of my heart.

"Jesus, confirm my heart's desire,
    To work, and speak, and think, for Thee;
Still let me guard the holy fire,
    And still stir up Thy gift in me."

Meditation

"Of far greater service than any array of learning or gifts of eloquence, . . . or apparent opportunities for large usefulness, of deeper significance than high intellectual attainment, or power of popular influence, is this gift—may God give it to each of us!—the secret and sweetness of unceasing, prevailing, triumphant prayer for the kingdom of the Lord Jesus Christ."— *Robert E. Speer.*

My Temple

There's a temple I know in the heart of the woods,
    Where the wood bird sings its sweet song,
And a silence, aware with the fragrance of prayer,
    Is lingering all the day long.

There wood flowers worship in reverence profound
    In this living cathedral of mine,
And the winds wafting by, lift their prayers to the sky,
    To the God of this temple divine.

A brook tumbles down through this temple I know,
    O'er its altars of moss and of stone,
And it chants all the day in a soft solemn way,
    To the God who is there Lord alone.

Sweet music is there in the heart of the woods,
    And he who is listening hears
A breathing of peace, a soul's sweet release,
    And the thoughts that lie deeper than tears.

So take me away to the heart of the woods,
    Where the temples are made without hands;
With the birds and the breeze and the tall towering trees,
    Let me worship—*my heart understands!*

II

PRAY YE THEREFORE

"Pray ye therefore the Lord of the harvest" (Matthew 9. 38).

We must think some more upon this command to make prayer our first work. We must fix Jesus' words in our minds—"Pray ye therefore."

> "Prayer is the soul's sincere desire,
>   Unuttered or expressed,
> The motion of a hidden fire
>   That trembles in the breast."

Hidden fire! How did we first get acquainted with this "hidden fire"? We are learning what Pentecost at the beginning taught our church Fathers, that there could be no fire to "tremble in the breast" until prayer had first opened the way. "Tarry ye" was the first command. And because they obeyed and "continued in prayer and supplication" the "power" came and Jerusalem was stirred.

"Pray ye therefore." Why the "therefore"? Is not the answer to be found in two facts?—first, the stupendous greatness of the tasks before the disciple of Christ, and, second, his utter helplessness to do anything about it if left to himself. "Pray ye therefore."

The late James W. Bashford of China furnishes an illustration of the meaning of these words. Other missionaries have told the same story. Face to face with the terrible needs of the people of that vast country, Bashford was staggered. He saw how "humanly impossible" was the task before him. "Therefore," he said in describing the emergency to a fellow worker, "I made up my mind that I could not depend upon my friends in America, that I must depend upon God alone. Therefore, I must live closer to God than I had ever done before. I must get into the very heart of God!"

> Into the heart of God! Show me the way;
> Within the heart of God, there let me stay.
> Thou art so weak, my soul, burdens so sore;
> Into the heart of God, more and still more!

These "desperate situations" that, sooner or later,

come to all of us either make us or break us. One who
has at least once in a lifetime "prayed through" will
have behind him a great experience that will be to him
ever a source of strength and hope. Afterwards he
will know that prayer changes things.

One such experience came to Moses and Aaron and
Hur upon a hilltop in Rephidim. That desperate
prayer meeting on the hill was the deciding factor in
the battle upon the plain. When it was over, "The
Lord said unto Moses, Write this for a memorial in
a book" (Exodus 17. 14). And he did.

Israel needed to remember that prayer meeting, just
as we do. The battle was fierce that day, and the crisis
was near. The results would be far-reaching in the
history of the chosen people. So while Joshua was
leading the battle in the valley, Moses and Aaron and
Hur were in the midst of a great spiritual conflict
upon the hilltop alone with God.

When these three ceased in their intercession Israel
was driven. And the final victory came only when
they learned—what God wanted them to learn—that
the intercession that lays hold of the spiritual forces
of Heaven, is the decisive factor in the victories of all
the years. "Write this for a memorial in a book."
"Pray ye therefore."

* * *

A Prayer

O Thou Saviour of the world, awaken us. Forgive
our sins, yes, forgive our sins. But oh, the sin of the
world! Awaken us to the sin of the world, the dull-
ing, deadening sins that grip our world. Help us to
get this world upon our hearts. It is such a needy
world of broken minds and hearts and bodies. O

God, forgive us that so often we have forgotten Thy world. May Thy Kingdom come and Thy will be done on earth. Amen.

Meditation

"Is intercession a travail, or is it a playtime, a recreation, the least exacting of all things, an exercise in which there is neither labor nor blood? 'The blood is the life.' Bloodless intercession is dead. It is only the man whose prayer is a vital expenditure, a sacrifice which holds fellowship with Calvary, who 'fills up that which is behind in the sufferings of Christ.' "— *J. H. Jowett.*

Evening and Morning and Noon

I met Him at evening when work was done
And told Him the things I had lost and won;
And there at the close of a hard day's race
I met the Master face to face!

We talked of those things I had won and lost,
And He stilled a soul that was tempest-tossed;
But in that hour I heard Him say,
"My son, you should find me at break of day."

So I met Him there in the morning light,
And gone were the shadows and burdens of night,
As strongly He sent me out of that place,
Where I met the Master face to face.

But, lo, in the midst of the noonday heat
I stumbled and lost the Presence sweet,
And ashamed, in that hour I heard Him say:
"My son, you must seek me at noon of day.

"For the evening and morning are not enough,
The day is long and the road is rough.
As the heat increases strong men grow weak;
New strength from above your soul must seek."

And that's how I learned at the noon of the day
To lift mine eyes and steal away,
At least in thought, to some quiet place,
Where I sit with the Master face to face!

III

A CRUCIAL HOUR

"But we will continue steadfastly in prayer" (Acts 6. 4, A. R. V.).

It seems evident that the most stupid heresy in the Christian Church has nothing to do with theological controversy. Sadly enough, it has to do with this more vital matter of prayer. Insofar as the Church of today does not share the conviction of the early Church— that prayer is the first work—just so far we are in danger not only of becoming practical atheists, but also of blocking Christ's program for the evangelization of the world.

It was a very crucial hour in the history of the Church when "the twelve called the multitude of the disciples unto them." The occasion was the announcement of a very important decision.

A great peril had arisen in the rapidly growing church in Jerusalem. Problems of administration had become serious. Among the other things that threatened the life of the new "fellowship" was the "murmuring of the Grecians against the Hebrews, because their widows were neglected in the daily ministrations" (Acts 6. 1).

So it developed that not only were racial problems threatening, but also the leaders of the church were in peril of being tangled up in the wheels of the machinery. Would the major emphasis be placed upon organization to the neglect of the spiritual resources?

We can well wish that the leaders of the Church in all generations could have seen as clearly as did those early leaders who took their stand upon the primacy of their stewardship of prayer. Accordingly, they refused to be taken from that secret place where God's resources are made available. They said, "Look ye out ... seven men of honest report, ... whom we may appoint over this business. But we will give ourselves continually to prayer, and to the ministry of the word."

Across the whole Church there is a vital need of recapturing this emphasis upon intercession as "the first work" of Christian leaders. I have counseled with groups of officials in many parts of America on this subject, and always with the same results. There is a perilous lack of attention to prayer and worship. In more than a score of questionnaires among groups of officials in various sections of the country the results are about the same as the following:

	Yes	No
1. Do you have family prayers?	32	54
2. Do you have grace at the table?	66	20
3. Do you keep the quiet hour or morning watch?	40	46
4. Do you think you should?	82	2
5. Do you read the Bible at least once a week?	60	25
6. Do you read the Bible daily?	32	54
7. Is the prayer meeting in your weekly schedule?	21	65

While this questionnaire is among the best I have found, there is real ground for concern. Think of officials in the Church who have no "blessing" at the table, who have no daily quiet hour with Christ, who feel no responsibility for the midweek worship! Listen to Andrew Murray, "If the amount of true wrestling with God in the daily life of the average Christian could be disclosed, the wonder might be, not that he accomplishes so little, but that God is willing to use him at all."

Do we not see a need for a new campaign, not for money, but for holy habits? Where are the laymen who will lead a movement to "make the Sabbath different," to establish daily prayer and Bible reading in the home, to build the fires of prayer underneath the Church?

I know how busy and how weary laymen get these days, but I also know how Sunday-night parties are increasing everywhere. And the same thing is true of the night of the midweek service. It surely is time for someone to start a Loyalty League for laymen who will promise to be at worship—or at home—*or nowhere else!* We simply must keep up these holy habits or we are lost. Vital church membership and comradeship with Christ are impossible on any other basis.

* * *

A Prayer

Dear Heavenly Father, grant us wisdom for this day. Thou hast created us and redeemed us. Thy love is from everlasting to everlasting; we would rest in Thee. Grant that all our resources of mind and heart and will may be dedicated anew this day to the advancement of Thy kingdom. Through Jesus Christ our Lord. Amen.

Meditation

Jesus went into the synagogue on the Sabbath day "as his custom was." And Daniel continued to pray three times a day "as he did afore time." Unless a thing is done with regularity it is done with difficulty.

For instance, "Desultory church attendance is hard. One has to fight a battle every Sunday, and no one is strong enough to survive an ordeal like that. Let a person once decide that church-going deserves a fixed place in the schedule of his week's life, and the battle is won."

Steeple Climbers

Many times I've heard the story,
How one day the God of glory
Told a priest up in the steeple,
"I'm down here among my people!"

Well, perhaps there are some preachers,
With a kind of wooden features,
Who must get right down to earth
'Ere they come to be of worth;

But as I have viewed the people,
Priests and all, they need a steeple!
Or some other quiet place
Where men climb to see God's face.

Friend of man, keep close to earth,
But you'll never be of worth,
You will never lift the people
Till you learn to climb the steeple!

IV

NOTHING BUT PRAYER

"Lord, I believe; help thou mine unbelief" (Mark 9. 24).

Nothing but prayer! No, nothing but prayer can do what Jesus did in today's scripture. At least this is the explanation which the Master gave His disciples of their own failure to heal the epileptic boy.

"You must pray more!" That was really what Jesus said as, later, they huddled about Him in their private quarters. "Why couldn't we cast it out?" they had asked.

As one reads this human-interest story, with the quick transition from the mysteries of the Mount of Transfiguration down into the valley of human tragedy, where Jesus' disciples suffered defeat, one feels like saying,

"O for a faith that will not shrink,
Though pressed by every foe,
That will not tremble on the brink
Of any earthly woe!"

We can easily see and feel the various scenes in that drama. First, the hopeful father, who, out of great love for his sick boy, had brought him to the disciples of Jesus. Then the brave but untrained attempt at healing; followed by the terrible disappointment of the parent and the chagrin of the disciples. How often we have felt as they did when we have failed! What is the reason?

And then comes Jesus upon the scene, fresh from the transfiguration; the light of heaven is still upon His face, so that the people are "amazed." In a moment the heartbroken father has confronted the Master. His sick son is with him—and the humiliated disciples. And as the crowds begin to gather, Jesus takes it all in.

Life is like that! We all go at times from the high places down into the valley. But the saddest thing about the valley places is the disappointments. So it was with Jesus—disappointment over His disciples' failure. How slow they are to learn! "O faithless generation, how long shall I be with you?" What do these words mean? If we could understand better what they mean, we should know better the secret of prevailing prayer.

I have before me a statement by Mr. Roger Babson, in which he says, "Thomas Edison's last words to me, shortly before his death, were, 'Babson, my belief is that God will not let this nation advance much more materially until it catches up spiritually.'"

But how slow we are catching up spiritually! How little progress we make! That was what Jesus sorrowed over twenty centuries ago as He saw His disciples defeated in their attempt to appropriate the spiritual resources of God. "Bring him to me," Jesus cried. "All things are possible to those who believe."

And the yearning father answered back in trembling words, "I believe, help thou mine unbelief!"

Now, the lesson that speaks to us out of this pathetic story is that we need to pray more if we are not to disappoint Christ. Again and again He says, "Pray ye the Lord of the harvest." "Hitherto ye have asked nothing in my name. Pray." And, "Verily I say unto you, If ye have faith as a grain of mustard seed, . . . nothing shall be impossible unto you" (Matthew 17. 20).

These commands of our Lord to pray are the more urgent because He practiced them Himself. He faced all the difficulties that we face in maintaining communion with the Heavenly Father. But His first precaution was always to keep clear the lines of communication that led above. On this point Dr. Robert E. Speer writes, "There are two things which make our Lord's example in the life of prayer of special significance. In the first place, if ever anyone could have dispensed with prayer, it was He. In the second place, His experience tried out the whole reality of prayer. Whatever He found in it, we may be sure is there."

A Prayer

Dear living Lord, help us to believe. Help us to believe that God is waiting to reveal to us the possibilities of prayer. Give us a new faith in the unreleased resources of Heaven. O teach us to pray, but first help us to determine that we will pray. In Jesus' name. Amen.

Meditation

"Allow no rush of work or of pleasure to crowd out time for prayer. Luther once said, 'I have much work to do today, so I will arise an hour earlier in order to have time for quiet prayer.' Those who make a rule of the Morning Watch should resolve never to allow a single exception. Cling unshakably to the regular observance of this life-giving habit."—*David R. Porter.*

The Secret

I met God in the morning
    When my day was at its best,
And His presence came like sunrise,
    Like a glory in my breast.

All day long the Presence lingered,
    All day long He stayed with me,
And we sailed in perfect calmness
    O'er a very troubled sea.

Other ships were blown and battered,
    Other ships were sore distressed,
But the winds that seemed to drive them,
    Brought to us a peace and rest.

Then I thought of other mornings,
    With a keen remorse of mind,
When I too had loosed the moorings,
    With the Presence left behind.

So I think I know the secret,
  Learned from many a troubled way:
You must seek Him in the morning
  If you want Him through the day!

V

THE UNSEEN LEADER

"Without me ye can do nothing" (John 15. 5).

The fifteenth chapter of John's Gospel could be called the countryman's chapter. Jesus never could have spoken these words had He not been familiar with vineyards and fruit trees and the great out of doors. In the background of this nature portrait is the countryman's conviction that a barren fruit tree or barren grapevine is a useless thing.

The lesson which the Master is here teaching is that the steward of God, like a fruit tree, is expected to bear fruit. If not, he has missed his calling. How many disciples of Jesus have never understood this!

"To serve the present age,
  My calling to fulfill;
O may it all my powers engage
  To do my Master's will!"

But Jesus connects fruit-bearing with prayer. It is a remarkable statement, "Ye shall ask what ye will, and it shall be done unto you" (John 15. 7). Think of it. "Ask what ye will"—the achievements of the prayer-steward are unlimited in possibilities. Yet how little we have explored this field!

But in order to find the secret of prevailing prayer and efficient fruit-bearing we must remember the Master's two prior statements: "Without me ye can do nothing" (15. 5); and second, "If ye abide in me, and

my words abide in you" (15. 7). Then comes the
promise, "Ye shall ask what ye will."

Evidently, there is an "Unseen Leader" behind the
curtain without whom "ye can do nothing"; the first
business of the prayer-steward is to abide in Him; *and
for the high purpose of bearing fruit for the Kingdom.*
Thus this fifteenth chapter of John's Gospel will reveal
to our careful meditation the reason for much of our
failure in prayer.

Evidently, one of the main purposes of prayer is to
help us to *do something*. Of course prayer is indispensable to the Christian's own joy in Christ, but
nevertheless this fellowship with Him will surely fade
out unless there grows the conviction within us that
prayer at its best is prayer for Kingdom conquest. We
have something to do besides the getting of joy and
strength for our own souls.

> "Nothing to do! Thou Christian soul,
> Wrapping thee 'round in thy selfish stole,
> Off with the garments of sloth and sin,
> Christ, thy Lord, hath a kingdom to win."

What Jesus is really teaching us in this scripture is
that the faithful prayer-steward both brings joy and
power to himself, and, by his intercession, releases the
resources of Christ upon the needy world about him.

Said George Muller: "It has pleased the Lord to
teach me a truth, the benefit of which I have not lost,
for more than fourteen years. The point is this: I saw
more clearly than ever that the first great and primary
business to which I ought to attend every day was to
have my soul happy in the Lord."

Lest these words be misunderstood, note the following lines, which indicate that this prayer-steward is

fundamentally concerned for his fruit bearing. He adds: "For I might seek to set the truth before the unconverted, I might seek to benefit believers, I might seek to relieve the distressed, I might in other ways seek to behave myself as it becomes a child of God in this world, and yet, not being happy in the Lord, and not being nourished and strengthened in my inner man day by day, all this might not be attended to in the right spirit."

How many there are of us who desperately need this lesson! Indeed, there is a vast number of professing Christians who do not get much enthusiasm out of singing,

"Sweet hour of prayer, sweet hour of prayer,
That calls me from a world of care,"

who would have their prayer periods transformed if they would widen their horizons. They would find a new fellowship with the Presence if they would add to their now narrow petitions, for themselves and their own little circle, a passion for their neighbors and the whole wide world which Christ came to save!

* * *

A Prayer

"Lord, speak to me, that I may speak
    In living echoes of Thy tone;
As Thou hast sought, so let me seek
    Thy erring children, lost and lone.

.   .   .   .

"O use me, Lord, use even me
    Just as Thou wilt, and when, and where,
Until Thy blessed face I see,
    Thy rest, Thy joy, Thy glory share."
                    —*Frances Ridley Havergal.*

Meditation

"If your acts of prayer are the most regular things in your life, I think you will find that they regulate all else. I cannot imagine a person who is regular in prayer being unpunctual in anything. It is the regular use of prayer which leads to spontaneity."—*Dr. W. E. Orchard.*

Aldersgate

What is this unseen Presence that commands me,
    That grips my mind and will not turn away?
Sure as the dawn a Holy One approaches
    Upon my spirit each returning day!

Ofttimes I tell myself 'tis but illusion,
    And doubting ask how such a thing could be:
A Voice that speaks beyond our human hearing,
    A Presence eyes of flesh can never see?

And then again it comes, a warming Nearness,
    Comes with a strengthening, a courage, and a cheer,
Comes until all my futile doubts are doubted,
    Comes until Heaven is the Here!

Oh, it must be this Presence is the Christ-One,
    He who once said: "I will come back to you;
Unseen, the blinded world will never know me;
    But ye shall know as long as ye are true."

O living Christ, Lord of the whole creation,
    O living Word, through every age the same,
Jesus the Christ, today, yes, and forever,
    A thousand ages bless Thy holy name!

VI

Prayer Bowls

"Each with his harp and with golden bowls full of incense (that is, full of *the prayers* of the saints), *singing a new song*" (Revelation 5. 8, 9, Moffatt).

Golden bowls full of prayers of the saints! And harps. And the inhabitants of heaven singing a new song. And then something happening on earth. What does it all mean?

Whatever else the "golden bowls" in Revelation may mean, this much seems certain: here is a figurative attempt to teach that the prayers of "the saints" are faithfully preserved before the throne of God.

Real praying is never a waste of energy or of time. Prayer is the divinely ordained means by which the sons of God may share with the Father the control of world forces. At last, when the "prayer bowls" are filled, some heavenly angel adds fire to "the prayers of the saints" and something happens on earth, "voices, and thunderings, and lightnings, and an earthquake" (Revelation 8. 5).

Professor John Alfred Faulkner, of Drew University, has preserved for us a private memorandum made by a missionary pastor on whom the picture of the "prayer bowls" in heaven had made a deep impression.

The following is one of the paragraphs: "I became pastor of a church, and started to get something into the prayer vials. It was a broken-down church, for it had never been broken up. There were ten godly women, but they were reviled, and the church was a byword. We gave one evening each week to nothing but prayer. God saw the measure which He required, and when the vials of prayer were full, He poured them out. We did not have altar services because the whole place was an altar. There was the pouring down of God's convincing Spirit. The whole community was turned upside down, which meant right side up, and I had the joy of receiving many into the assembly. Those tall, strong men were gloriously transformed by the same graces, by the revelation of Jesus Christ."

That suggestion of filling up the "prayer bowls" must be a good one. Always remember that it is figurative language and that prayer is more than "incense" set afire; but we must also remember that here is a great exhortation to keep on praying. We are to keep on praying in spite of all the mysteries involved. Jesus never tried to explain prayer; He commanded it. Neither did He explain mysteries of the spiritual birth, but He did say, "Ye must be born again." Ye must!

Why should we be troubled by the mysterious any longer, after we have become accustomed to much that is at present unexplainable? "Knowledge and mystery have a habit of dwelling together, but the mystery does not invalidate the fact." Recently a great scientist declared that "the best of the scientists know that we are little kindergarten fellows playing with mysteries!"

The world is full of the unexplainable, and Jesus never tried to explain. He just kept urging His disciples to explore the undiscovered secrets of the spiritual universe. He just kept on telling them that God is a Father. "If ye then, being evil, know how to give good gifts unto your children, how much more shall your Father which is in heaven give good things to them that ask him?" (Matthew 7. 11.)

Oh, why don't we pray, pray, pray? Prayer is the heaven-given means by which the disciple of Christ is to release, in His Name, the resources and energies of God. "When I shall see Christians all over the world resolved to prove what shall be the efficacy of prayer for the conversion of the world, I shall begin to think that the millennium is at the door."

And Robert E. Speer adds to the above quotation, "Deeper than the needs of men; deeper far than the need for money; aye, deep down at the bottom of our spiritless life, is the need of the forgotten prevailing world-wide prayer."

* * *

A Prayer

O Thou living God, teach us to pray. Help us first of all to hear Thy call to prayer. May the need of the world bring us to our knees, until we shall feel ourselves to be channels of Thy grace. O give us the resolve to pray; morning, noon, and night, teach us to pray. In Christ's dear name. Amen.

Meditation

"Moral force has before it dramatic opportunities in mass prayer. Suppose in every country in the world five minutes were set aside at noon each day for a week in which all work except absolute necessities were stopped while people bowed their heads and asked God to help free the world from the yoke of men who would exploit their fellow human beings?"—*David Lawrence.*

Frightened Child

Whenever I hear in the nighttime
　　The cry of a child in fear,
Just wanting to know in his darkness
　　Only this—that his mother is near,

Then I think of the longing within me,
　　How I yearn, wherever I stand,
For the Voice that speaks in my darkness,
　　And the clasp of my Father's hand!

For sometimes the shadows surround me
　　And I am the frightened child,
With the tempest howling about me,
　　And the storm in my heart growing wild,

Then my fear would increase to terror
Were it not that where'er I may be,
It is mine to feel for my comfort
That my Father is ever near me!

VII

The Master-Teacher

"Lord, teach us to pray" (Luke 11. 1).

Jesus is the Master-Teacher of the prayer-steward.
If one really purposes to explore the secrets of prevailing prayer, he will go to Jesus.

Andrew Murray points out this significant fact that
Jesus talked more to His disciples about prayer than
about preaching. It is probable too that Jesus spent
less time in preaching than in prayer.

Moreover, I think the same could be shown to be
true of the great Christian preachers of every century.
First of all they prayed. They not only talked about
prayer, but they prayed. Yes, they learned to listen to
the voice of the Father.

"Father, I stretch my hand to Thee;
No other help I know!"

One of the most striking things about the Scripture
passages where Jesus is either in prayer or is teaching
prayer is His evident nearness to the Spirit-Presence.
In the closing days of His ministry, at a very crucial
moment when He stands before the closed tomb of
the dead Lazarus, in intimate and victorious communion, we hear Him say, "Father, I thank thee that
thou hast heard me. And I knew that thou hearest me
always." Is not this the high peak of praying to be
able to say, "I know that Thou hearest me always"?

It must have been a wonderful experience to have heard Jesus pray. Therefore it is not strange that one of His disciples should have said to Him, "Lord, teach *us* to pray." "And it came to pass that as he was praying in a certain place, when he ceased, one of his disciples said to him, Lord, teach us to pray."

Thus it happened that the great Teacher gave to His disciples His master-teaching on prayer and intercession. We call it the Lord's Prayer. Without doubt it is the most important key to effective praying that exists anywhere in the world.

But Jesus had given them this prayer pattern before! In the Sermon on the Mount we find it. Did they remember that day, nearly a year before, when the Lord had said, "After this manner pray ye"?

In the Sermon on the Mount Jesus had emphasized one great lesson: "When ye pray, use not vain repetitions, as the heathen do; for they think that they shall be heard for their much speaking." We need that lesson too. "Be not ye therefore like unto them," given to "much speaking." We need to do less speaking and more listening. Yes, and more thinking. Have you ever spent half an hour with the Lord's Prayer? Alone with yourself and Him? Saying over and over again those wonderful words, "Our Father." None but Jesus had ever dared to call Jehovah "Father." God is love. He has the same feeling toward us that an earthly father has toward his children. And every phrase in the Lord's Prayer is rich in secret meaning. But first, there is the prayer for the Kingdom: "Thy kingdom come, thy will be done on earth." How few take it to heart and yet it is the very heart of the prayer. "On earth!" Jesus said. "Thy will be done on *earth*."

Then there comes the petition for our own daily needs, "Give us this day our daily bread." Evidently, our Father expects us to come to Him with all our daily needs. In that same Sermon on the Mount Jesus had said, "Your heavenly Father knoweth that ye have need of all these things. Seek ye first the kingdom of God and his righteousness, and all these things shall be added unto you" (Matthew 6. 32, 33). Here notice one important condition of prevailing prayer. "The kingdom" comes *first*. "Seek ye first the kingdom," said Jesus. Yes, even before our own needs come the needs of the Kingdom.

Andrew Murray says on this point: "I feel sure that as long as we look on prayer chiefly as the means of maintaining our own Christian life, we shall not know fully what it is meant to be. But when we learn to regard it as the highest part of the work entrusted to us, the root and strength of all other work, we shall see that there is nothing we shall so need to study and practice as the art of praying aright."

And, finally, what else do those closing words of the Lord's Prayer teach if not that God intends us to expect that our prayers will be answered? *"For thine is the kingdom, and the power, and the glory, for ever. Amen."*

* * *

A Prayer

Lord Jesus, teach me also to pray. Quicken my will at this moment, that I may deeply purpose to enroll in Thy school of prayer. Help me to make this my first work, that I may know Thee the living Christ, to the glory of Thy holy name. Amen.

Meditation

"God loves you not because you are clever, not because you are good, but because He is *your Father*. The Cross of Christ does not make God love us; it is the outcome and measure of His love to us. He loves all His children, the dullest, the worst of His children. His love lies at the back of everything, and we must get upon that as the solid foundation of our religious life. We must begin there or our beginning will come to nothing."—*Mark Guy Pearse*.

Voice of God

(After meditating on "Renascence")

God, I don't have to push apart
The grass to feel Thy beating heart!
For while I keep me pure from sin
I feel Thee breathing deep within,
And by the gift of Thy sweet grace
I hear Thee whisper face to face.

I know not how such things can be,
But I do know He speaks with me,
Not from the grass nor from the sod,
But in my heart the Voice of God,
Speaking Spirit unto spirit;
Oh, if I listen I can hear it,
Voice of God that calls to me
Out of His infinity!

CHAPTER SEVEN

The Major Peril

I

THE MASTER WARNS

"If therefore ye have not been faithful in the unrighteous mammon, who will commit to your trust the true riches?" (Luke 16. 11.)

IN a previous chapter we began to meditate upon "the leaks" of life, the leaks that prevent one from being "filled with all the fullness of God." Accordingly, we have been pondering over carelessness with time and prayer. And now we come to perhaps the major peril facing the Christian steward.

Certainly, Jesus startles one with what He has to say about money and property. How much good these can do on the one hand; and, on the other, the peril that money brings! Read this story of the unrighteous steward.

Is it any wonder, when one considers the peril that comes with wealth, that a wise man prayed, "Give me neither poverty nor riches"? And Jesus' word here is simply tremendous in its implications: "If therefore ye have not been faithful with money, how can you ever be trusted with true riches?"

In the first place Jesus warns that money is not true riches. The Christian ought to be sure of this, so sure that he will not covet money. But all of us need money! And all of us will have to handle it along the way in our quest for the true riches of life. Therefore Jesus

162

makes the plain warning that the true riches—the supreme quest of life—will never be found if we allow money to tempt us into unfaithfulness along the by-paths.

Therefore, the getting and the use of money and property is a most vital matter in which the Christian needs to check himself constantly. Is Christ ruling on this throne, or have the pagan gods the right of way? Probably more of us deceive ourselves in the presence of mammon than before any other idol throne. This was why John Wesley was so plain-spoken in an old sermon that has come down to us.

He says: "Some of you Methodists are twice as rich as you were before you were Methodists; some of you are fourfold as rich; some of you are tenfold as rich; now, if, whilst you get all you can and save all you can, you do not give all you can, then you are tenfold more the child of hell than you were before."

What is behind such urgency on Wesley's part? He explains, "Christianity has in it the elements of its own destruction." "When a man becomes a true Christian he becomes industrious, trustworthy, and prosperous. Now, if that man, whilst he gets all he can and saves all he can, does not give all he can, I have more hope of Judas Iscariot than of that man!"

Dr. Walter Rauschenbusch was once asked, What is the greatest contribution which a man can make to a new social order? He answered, "A regenerated personality." But, unfortunately, regeneration doesn't seem generally to get down to the pocketbook. Either the religious education was not full enough or the consecration was not deep enough.

I profoundly believe that the money which belongs by every right to God, but is held back from Him by

His professed followers, constitutes the greatest hindrance to vital spiritual life that there is in the world today.

Now all of this is forewarned in the Scriptures. Riches in themselves are not condemned, but continually we are warned against the setting of the heart upon them. Money can become a rival god. So Jesus warns, "If therefore ye have not been faithful in the unrighteous mammon, who will commit to your trust the true riches?"

Now, no one can afford to deal carelessly with this warning from our Lord. Some of His hearers tried to do so on that long-ago day: "Now the Pharisees, who were fond of money, heard all this, and they sneered at him. So he told them, 'You are the people who get men to think you are good, but God knows what your hearts are!'" (Luke 16. 14, 15, Moffatt.)

* * *

A Prayer

"Almighty God, from whom all good things come; give Thy grace, we humbly beseech Thee, to those whom Thou hast entrusted with riches; that they, as faithful stewards, may dispense them in the service of Thy kingdom for the increase thereof; to the honor and praise of Him, who, though He was rich, yet for our sakes became poor, Thy Son, Jesus Christ, our Lord. Amen."—*Bishop Wilbur P. Thirkield.*

Meditation

"To reach old age, possessed only of money and a desire to increase it, is not success in life. It is a sad and terrible failure; better die a pauper in purse than a pauper in soul; better fail to get money than to allow money to get you."—*Unknown*.

Profit and Loss

I counted dollars while God counted crosses,
I counted gains while He counted losses!
I counted my worth by the things gained in store,
But He sized me up by the scars that I bore.
I coveted honors and sought for degrees;
He wept as He counted the hours on my knees.
And I never knew till one day by a grave,
How vain are these things that we spend life to save.
Yes, I never knew until Jim went above,
That the richest of all in the world is God's love!

II

MONEY TALK

"He who is faithful with a trifle is also faithful with a large trust" (Luke 16. 10, Moffatt).

Let us linger longer with this very illuminating sixteenth chapter of St. Luke's Gospel. We ought to get fixed in our minds the main points of Jesus' "money talk." And we must remember that the Pharisees sneered at Him! Do we join with them or with those wiser souls who insist that what the Pharisees called a "trifling matter" is at the very heart of the problem? The money test has to do both with our fellowship with the living Christ and with the building of His kingdom. Well, suppose we face this challenge that "money talk" is a trifling matter. Jesus' first reply is that *He who is faithful with a trifle is also faithful with a large trust.* Have we ever thought of that? Do we not reveal our true character by the way we handle the little things, the commonplace things? There are those who believe you can tell a man by his speech. The young woman said to Peter upon that tragic night when Jesus' disciples "followed afar off," "Thy speech bewrayeth thee" (Matthew 26. 73).

In more than one way that is the truth. I well remember in my early ministry in a city church in Massachusetts how the treasurer came to the minister at the close of the morning sermon in which he had referred to money-giving. Putting his hand affectionately upon the preacher's shoulder, he said: "Pastor, let me give you some advice. Don't talk money from the pulpit. People will think that you are after their money. Don't do it."[1]

Why should a minister *not* give "money talks"? Jesus did. Very many of them. O that we might do it as wisely and as skillfully as He did! We must learn how, for so often we bungle the business. And it is most important—not merely to get people's money but to get their money *and them.*

Returning to the New England treasurer: I well remember that night when his theory of silence on money talk was shown to be worthless. It was the final business meeting of the year. The treasurer had reported the annual deficiency. And then, *as in former years,* the officials proceeded to make plans for the annual "Agony Sunday." It was more than the new pastor could endure. "Brothers," he said, "this is a sorry business. We can't afford to spoil our Sunday services by what seems to me to be neither a dignified nor a worshipful performance. Any one of a half a dozen of you men could pay this entire deficiency and hardly feel it. But the saddest part is, that we have

---

[1] See *An Explanation,* p. 215.

been so unbusinesslike in conducting the Lord's business. If any of you men were to run your own affairs in the way you have been carrying on the Lord's business, you would fail in a short time, and you would deserve to."

When the pastor sat down, there was silence, until William Winters, a banker, rose to his feet. The words that he spoke have never been forgotten by the pastor of that church.

"It seems to me," he said, "that our minister has hit the nail on the head. I certainly think that we ought to be ashamed that we have not conducted the Lord's affairs in a more businesslike manner." Hesitating a little, he continued: "However, I think it is only fair to add that it is the fault of the pastors who have served this church."

The minister swallowed, and the banker went on. "I have been a member here for thirty years," he said. "I have been a fairly regular attendant, but only twice during these years have I heard a sermon which made any reference whatever to the vital relation that exists between the paying of our money and the consecration of our lives." Then there was another hesitation. And it was not in bitterness that he added: "And neither of those sermons was preached by our present pastor." It is needless to say that the minister went home to look up his record.

Jesus never dodged the money question. He was constantly educating on this subject. Many students of the gospel declare that He had more to say about a man's attitude toward money and property than about any other one thing. In any case it is certainly significant that in sixteen of his thirty-eight parables Jesus has made this His theme. We ought to search out

those passages of Scripture for ourselves and see that
Jesus makes it perfectly clear that money-giving is both
a way to and an expression of the consecration of life.

* * *

A Prayer

O Thou Divine Dweller of hearts, I worship Thee.
Who am I that Thy Spirit wouldst come and dwell
with my spirit, in this house of clay? May no sin of
mine drive Thee thence. O Christ of my heart, I pray
Thee to guide and guard me, that my dealings with
the world this day may be acceptable in Thy sight.
Amen.

Meditation

"The most sensitive spot in the surrender of the
whole life to God is my property. Perhaps it is because property provides me with material comforts,
selfish satisfactions, and gratifies personal tastes and
appetites. . . . The question is, Who is owner—God or
myself? If God, then I must surrender all to Him.
Always man has attempted to except his property
from the surrender; but when I begin to condition my
surrender, then I begin to compromise; and to compromise with God is fatal to my soul."—*Bishop Theo-
dore S. Henderson.*

Like Summer Seas

(After reading "The Tempest," by Doctor Orchard)

Like summer seas that soothe the lonely shore,
  Like whispering winds that kiss the forest sod,
Like the still voice we cherish more and more,
  So is Thy coming unto us, dear God.

Like ships storm-driven from the sea,
  Like starving souls that seek the bread of life,
So is our coming, Saviour, unto Thee,
  Famished in soul and driven by the strife.

Like flowers that lift their faces to the day,
  Like trees that stalwart stand through years of storm,
So might our lives have been along the way;
  Had we but held in view that nobler Form.

But, like the sun that gilds with golden light,
  And warms the world with promise ever new,
So is Thy sweet returning, and Thy might
  To help us do the things we ought to do!

III

ETERNAL INVESTMENTS

"I tell you, use mammon, dishonest as it is, to make friends for yourselves" (Luke 16. 9, Moffatt).

The sixteenth chapter of Saint Luke's Gospel again! We just can't leave this "money parable" until we have seen the main lesson that Jesus teaches.

The point of the parable is this: *Money properly invested in Christ's name and for His kingdom will bring eternal rewards to the investor.*

Think of arriving at the "pearly gates" and being greeted by somebody with shining face saying: "Welcome, I've been looking for you; I want to greet the man whose investment of his money changed my life and opened heaven to me!"

That is exactly what the revised version of this scripture teaches. Jesus said, "I tell you, use mammon, . . . to make friends for yourselves."

Where and when? The scripture answers: "So that when you die, they," the friends your money has made for you, "may welcome you into the eternal abodes" (Moffatt).

Just think of this: Money can make friends for us! We have heard that before. "While I had money," said a disillusioned man, "I had plenty of friends." But here is something different—eternal friends; everlasting friendships!

Why don't we make better investments? Why don't we put our money where it will bring lasting dividends? Those are questions Jesus asked. Said He, "Why are 'the children of this world'—the grafters and the unjust stewards—wiser as respects their own generation than the children of the light?"

But there are examples of wise investors of money. In Florence, Italy, there is a tombstone which reads, "Here lies Estrella, who has gone to Heaven to enjoy a fortune of fifty thousand florins which she sent ahead in good deeds."

John Wesley might have been one of the richest men of his day. But all that came to him from the sale of his numerous publications went into Kingdom investments.

The last entry in Wesley's *Journal* was: "For upwards of eighty-six years I have kept my accounts exactly. I will not attempt it any longer, being satisfied with the continual conviction that I save all I can and give all I can, that is, all I have." He died a poor man; but think of the friends who awaited him at the pearly gates! "I tell you, use mammon, . . . to make friends for yourselves"—friends for eternity!

And there is another aspect to this matter. Not only may our giving change lives for time and eternity, but, "the quality of mercy is twice blessed." It brings new life and joy to the giver.

President A. C. Marts, of Bucknell University, after an extended study of present-day giving, recently declared that the happiest people in the world are those who share their income with others. But the evidence shows that they are far too few. "As a nation," he says, "we spend eighty-five per cent of our annual income, save twelve per cent, give only three per cent." We would be a vastly happier nation if we could be induced to give many times that three per cent. And the universe is on the side of such thinking. There is a profound spiritual law behind the truth that the sharing life not only saves my neighbor but saves me! On the other hand, all experience shows that the selfish pursuit of wealth never satisfies the craving of man's being—as Robert Service indicates,

"I wanted the gold, and I sought it;
    I scrabbled and mucked like a slave.
Was it famine or scurvy—I fought it;
    I hurled my youth into a grave.

"I wanted the gold, and I got it—
    Came out with a fortune last Fall—
Yet somehow life's not what I thought it,
    And somehow the gold isn't all."

* * *

A Prayer

"I am no longer my own, but Thine. Put me to what Thou wilt, rank me with whom Thou wilt; put me to doing, put me to suffering; let me be employed for Thee or laid aside for Thee, exalted for Thee or brought low for Thee; let me be full, let me be empty; let me have all things, let me have nothing; I freely and heartily yield all things to Thy pleasure and disposal.

"And now, O glorious and blessed God, Father, Son, and Holy Spirit, Thou art mine, and I am Thine. So be it. And the Covenant which I have made on earth, let it be ratified in heaven. Amen."—*The Wesley Covenant.*

𝔐𝔢𝔡𝔦𝔱𝔞𝔱𝔦𝔬𝔫

"Carlyle was forever insisting that the pursuit of wealth is not a 'human bond'; and Mr. J. L. Jacks, commenting, says: 'Seekers of buried treasure invariably quarrel among themselves for reasons which are manifest to a child. It makes no difference whether it is hidden in a pirate's cavern or in the bowels of the earth.'"—*Edwin M. Poteat.*

𝔏𝔦𝔣𝔢'𝔰 𝔉𝔲𝔩𝔣𝔦𝔩𝔩𝔪𝔢𝔫𝔱

Of all the prizes
That earth can give
   This is the best:
To find Thee, Lord,
A living Presence near,
   And in Thee rest!

Friends, fortune, fame,
   Of what might come to me—
I count all loss
If I find not
Companionship
   With Thee!

IV

The Unrealized Sin

"Keep yourselves from all covetousness" (Luke 12. 14).

The World War is now more than a generation behind us, but the terrible effects of that inhuman devastation will live forever. The cost might not have been too great if out of it the peoples of the earth had learned the futility of all wars.

One of the enduring sentences that came out of those war days was this, "Christianity has not been tried and found wanting—it has been found difficult and not tried." Gilbert K. Chesterton might have been writing an introduction to a plea for the Christianization of property and wealth. For not only is it true that the lust for profits was the underlying cause of the Great War, but this will be true of the next one also if it comes. The economic issues are the peril-issues in the world today, just as they always have been.

It is nearly twenty years since a prophetic voice wrote, "Have Western nations clean hands themselves when they condemn Japan's policy? . . . We have all got to repent together. . . . If Western nations do not repent of their godless gobbling of the world, let there be no pious preachments of 'Peace on earth, good will to men.' If selfishness is still to be in power, there will be war in the Far East, and when it comes, it will be a real war." And what the lust for dividends has been doing in the Orient it has also done for many years in many places. The race for business has been far-reaching and very demoralizing, a race carried out with cruel disregard for life and property in order that big commercial concerns might have the raw materials and markets at their own price.

Therefore perhaps the most neglected of all the commandments is the tenth, "Thou shalt not covet." Covetousness is stealing in the germ. Francis Xavier's warning has never been adequately heeded by the churchmen of any generation. We should meditate on these words, "I have had many people resort to me for confession. The confession of every sin that I have known or heard of, and of sins so foul that I never dreamed of them, has been poured into my ear. But no person has ever confessed to me the sin of covetousness."

We must begin at the house of God to fight this sin. A generation ago a prominent business man got excited over this matter. He said, "There is a sin in the Church that we are afraid to mention. We will tell you what its common name is and what its aristocratic name is and what its historic name is and what its spiritual name is. It is covetousness!"

"Oh, well," you say, "that is not so bad. That is a pretty white sort of sin—in fact, almost a virtue, for it is just saving—isn't it?—being thrifty and shrewd."

Then this Christian business man went on to say: "Well, listen to what Paul says about it: 'For this ye know of a surety, that no fornicator, nor unclean person, nor *covetous man,* who is an idolater, hath any inheritance in the kingdom of Christ and God' (Ephesians 5. 5).

"Now, that is awful. Surely Paul had gotten excited in speaking to the Ephesians. Surely, he did not mean that a man who simply hangs onto his world's goods should be classified in such frightful company as fornicators and idolaters. It must be that he was excited that day. Let us see what he said to the Colossians when he spoke to them: 'Put to death therefore your members which are upon the earth: fornication, uncleanness, passion, evil desire, and *covetousness,* which is idolatry (Colossians 3. 5).' "

So the business man went on into Romans and other scripture; then he concluded: "Here we are in this day of our Lord with a sin within our Church that is condemned more violently in the Scripture than any other sin. Search the Scripture from Genesis to Revelation, and you will not find the idolatry of Astoreth or Baal denounced in as lurid language as is this sin of covetousness. . . . Come, men of the Kingdom, let us talk about this thing!"

No wonder that Jesus said, "Keep yourselves from all covetousness: for a man's life consisteth not in the abundance of things which he possesseth" (Luke 12. 15).

* * *

A Prayer

"Search me, O God, and know my heart:
   Try me, and know my thoughts;
And see if there be any wicked way in me,
   And lead me in the way everlasting."
                    —Psalm 139. 23, 24, A. R. V.

Meditation

"The love that builds palatial homes and fills them with luxurious furnishings is not love for God or humanity. I do not envy homes built for family prestige. I tremble for their inmates lest they banish Christ, who loves the lowly, lonely, hungry, shivering, neglected ones. He allows comfort, but not luxury until all God's claims have been met, and never were more millions facing starvation than today right in the heart of Christendom. It is surely not God's time for building fortunes out of his bounty, or for the American people to be untrue to their stewardship of freedom and equal opportunities for all."—Bishop Earl Cranston.

A Hill-Born Prayer

From lust for gain or greed for gold,
   Keep me with high and holy mien;
But if the ships of fortune bring
   Some precious cargo clear and clean,
Safeguard me in my stewardship
   By glimpses of Thy great Unseen.

From lust for place or pomp or power,
  Save me with pure and passionate pride;
Curb not the hunger of my soul,
  But keep ambition sanctified.
Safeguard Thy steward, Lord, each day,
  By visions of Thy higher way.

V

A Page From Experience

"Neither will I offer . . . unto the Lord . . . that which doth cost me nothing" (2 Samuel 24. 24).

The burden of this present chapter is that Christianity has a money test. Jesus teaches this in the many parables and teachings of the New Testament, but it is also the witness of experience. It was an outspoken Kentucky physician who made the following assertion: *"You can tell the sincerity of a man's interest in anything by the way he puts his money into it."*

The physician was not a professing Christian. On the contrary, he was a severe critic of the Church. The ground of his criticism lay in the fact that he had met stingy and, in his judgment, dishonest church members. So out of his unfortunate experience he proceeded to make the generalization that church members as a class are stingy and, therefore, hypocritical. Thus he continued to reason until one day there came within his own horizon a young girl of heroic Christian spirit and simple devotion. With six others, this girl had joined in a covenant to pay one tenth of her income to the support of a struggling mission. It mattered not that her weekly wage was only three dollars and fifty cents. Nor did her faith waver because the income of her sick mother was pitifully small. God was calling and she followed. But at the end of the very first week she was in trouble. No one had told her that it was the *first* tenth of income that was to be set apart as "the first fruits" unto the Lord. On Saturday afternoon she went home sorrowful. Her week's bills had been paid, but of the tenth there remained only a few pennies for the mission. In her grief she threw herself down on her bed and wept. But no comfort came until a little pet dog—her only luxury—jumped up, with great show of sympathy, upon her bed. Then she remembered that a certain physician had made her a standing offer of twenty-five dollars for the pet. As she thought of it, a lump rose in her throat, and the struggle began in her heart. But the mission loomed large, and her covenant must not be broken. By night the physician owned the dog, and when the morning came, a young woman with a holy peace in her soul, and a glory in her face, laid the price of her sacrifice on the altar of the mission.

Years ago the Great Master had witnessed a similar act of sacrificial devotion, and He had said, "Wheresoever this gospel shall be preached throughout the whole world, this also that she hath done shall be spoken of for a memorial of her." And now it was not His will that the account of another young woman's devotion should be kept in a corner. Indeed, it was told in many a place, but in particular it came to the physician. It jarred him. Were there many more like her? Yes, there were six others who had made the same covenant! Then the physician pondered his philosophy, "You can tell the sincerity of a man's interest in anything by the way he puts his money into it." He was under conviction.

A few nights later, when the young lady came home from her work, a happy dog met her at the door.

Attached to his collar was an envelope containing a check for one hundred dollars! The Lord was at work in the physician's heart. A few weeks later the skeptic was converted, joined the Church of Christ, and became a loyal supporter of the mission. I have in my possession a photograph of that pet dog as he stood with the envelope attached to his neck. A perusal of the picture helps to prompt the question, Does religion have a money test?

A little meditation upon the story suggests that the average church member does not give enough to the Kingdom to keep himself spiritually healthy. David put this danger in remembered words when he said, "Neither will I offer ... unto the Lord ... that which doth cost me nothing."

> "Must Jesus bear the cross alone
> And all the world go free?
> No, there's a cross for every one,
> And there's a cross for me."

* * *

A Prayer

Not only my heart, dear Lord, but my mind needs Thee. Sanctify my mind by the enlightening power of Thy Holy Spirit. So being able to defeat the very beginnings of sin, may I be cleansed from all covetousness, to the glory of Jesus Christ our Lord. Amen.

Meditation

"Money is danger. We pass by too easily the searching warning words of Jesus. Nothing can fool men like money. It seems so powerful that it makes men forget the Supreme Power. It feeds pride until a man thinks he has no need of God. It constantly in-

vites selfishness. It commands so many things that
men forget the real goods which it can never purchase.
... There is only one way of escape: an evil master, it
can be a splendid workman; the minister of hell may
become a servant of light."—*Roger W. Babson.*

Dawn

Last night an angel met me at the door;
He said: "Time is no more;
I have been sent from heaven to say,
Tomorrow dawns for thee today;
Time will become Eternity,
Sleep thou tonight, tomorrow come with me."

And then I wept, my face unto the wall;
I heard a thousand earthly voices call,
Unfinished tasks, loved faces, children dear,
And in my soul I cried: "O leave me here!
Come not tomorrow, Angel, to my gate,
I crave more time; I pray thee wait!"

Then turned the angel with so sad a smile,
"Thou foolish one to pray to wait the while.
Open thine eyes! If thou couldst only see
The visions just beyond awaiting thee!
Wouldst thou abide where days dissolve in night?
How dull thou art to things beyond thy sight!"

VI

Not Empty-Handed

"None of you must appear before me empty-handed"
(Exodus 23. 15, Moffatt).

So religion does have a money test! And it was so
in the beginning. Jesus Himself made this plain, but
in doing so He simply reaffirmed the old principle that
a worshiper should not appear before the Lord "with
empty hands." The worship that is empty-handed is,

according to the Scriptures, simply not worship at all. The bringing of an offering to the altar of God is pictured in Scripture as a high and indispensable part of worship. Note carefully these three commands from the early days of Israel; the Lord Jehovah is speaking (Moffatt translation):

None of you must appear before me empty-handed (Exodus 23. 15).

All the first-born belong to me, with the firstlings of your cattle.... And none of you must appear before me empty-handed (Exodus 34. 19, 20).

Nor shall they appear before the Eternal empty-handed; every man must offer what he can afford, according as the Eternal your God has made you prosper" (Deuteronomy 16. 16, 17).

We must understand, in the first place, that the warning against empty-handed worship is primarily spoken for the sake of the worshiper. It is the worshiper who can't get along without giving. His soul-life is the thing at stake.

Anyone can test this truth by studying the inactive membership of any church. A member needs to pay in order to belong. When he stops his regular giving he begins to backslide. Of course his name may be on the records, but he really is not there himself unless he is subscribing and paying.

Worship dies that comes with empty hands, and presently it will not come at all. One of the main reasons why we have such a large list of unassimilated members in all of our churches is because we have failed in the duty of teaching regular and proportionate giving as a necessary part of worship. How can a church grow strong which allows a large percentage of its members to go along from year to year without making any subscription to the budget, or regularly participating in the holy act of presenting unto the Lord "tithes and offerings"?

Some great reasons lie behind this scripture demand that giving and worship be tied together. The first is that when a man gives his money he is giving himself and the way he gives his money is the way he gives himself.

A generation ago Dr. A. F. Schauffler made clear what we mean: "My definition of money is simply this: Money is myself. I am a laboring man, we will say, and can handle a pickax, and I hire myself out for a week at two dollars a day. At the close of the week I get twelve dollars, and I put it in my pocket. What is that twelve dollars? It is a week's worth of my muscle put into greenbacks and pocketed; that is, I have got a week's worth of myself in my pocket."

The quotation continues: "Now, the moment you understand this, you begin to understand that money in your pocket is not merely silver and gold, but it is something human, something that is instinct with power expended. Do you see what a blessed, what a solemn thing this giving is, this giving of my stored self to my Master?"

But the fundamental reason why no real worshiper can appear before God empty-handed is because money giving is the acknowledgment of two great principles of stewardship. First, *"God is the sovereign owner of all things."* And, second, *"Man is a steward and must account for that which is entrusted to him."*

Oh, that we could put reality into these two great principles! If only every church member could feel with the apostle Paul, "I have a stewardship entrusted to me"! If we could burn this word "stewardship" into our lives, then there would come to us a new sense of the reality of a personal God, and with this reality there would come new purpose and passion into our churches.

* * *

A Prayer

Blessed Christ, as Thou didst offer Thyself in loving sacrifice that we might be drawn to the Heavenly Father, so grant unto us such a measure of Thy Spirit, that we may be eager to deny ourselves for the Kingdom's sake and for the sake of Thy holy name. Amen.

Meditation

"My money is mine only in trust. It belongs to God, just as I do. This money is not filthy lucre. It is not the devil's coin. It is stored up human power. It is so much of myself which I can set at work in China or India or New York or Colorado. God is counting upon this money for His work."—*Harris Franklin Rall.*

All's Well

Sing, little yellow bird,
  Through the crisp air;
Summer is passing,
  We will not care.

Autumn is coming,
  Some will be sad;
Sing, little yellow bird,
  We will be glad.

Robin and bluebird,
  Repining, are still;
Sing, little yellow bird,
  Sing with a will.

Some will chant gaily
    In summer and spring;
We, little yellow bird,
    Ever will sing.

Dipping and singing,
    Flashing and bright,
God's tiny messenger;
    Everything's right!

VII

AFTER PENTECOST

"Not one of them considered anything his personal property" (Acts 4. 32, Moffatt).

"We give Thee but Thine own,
    Whate'er the gift may be;
All that we have is Thine alone,
    A trust, O Lord, from Thee."

The wonderful thing happened after Pentecost. Something that had never happened before. There came to pass a general recognition that God was the actual owner of all things! Other people had sung about it. "The earth is the Lord's, and the fullness thereof; the world, and they that dwell therein." Even as we sing rather carelessly,

"All things come of Thee, O Lord,
    And of Thine own have we given Thee."

But now for once, in the world's history, believers were so possessed by the spirit of a compelling stewardship that they were of one heart and of one soul, and *"neither said any of them that ought of the things which he possessed was his own."* But if those disciples didn't own what they possessed, who did? There are some who claim that in that early Church there was a sort of communism and all members owned things together. Not so! Doctor Moffatt's translation brings out the truth better, "They shared all they had with one another" (Acts 4. 32). It was Christians sharing with Christians! "There was not a needy person among them, for those who owned land or houses would sell them and bring the proceeds of the sale, laying the money before the feet of the apostles" (Acts 4. 34). No, it was not communism. At last there had appeared, following the fires of Pentecost, a real recognition that God is the owner of all things.

Many a man might come into a personal relation with the Father if he would learn to think of Him as the owner of his bank account and of his business and all his possessions. It ought to be easy to see why God is prevented from becoming real to those persons who will not let Him come into that most tangible realm of life, where we keep our material possessions. If we will not make God a partner here, why think of finding reality in the intangible world of the Spirit? Indeed, most of the essential doctrines of the Church stand in the same way, squarely on this double platform of God's sovereignty and of man's accountability. For instance we sing,

> "In my hand no price I bring;
> Simply to Thy cross I cling."

In these lines is the New Testament doctrine of salvation by faith—a precious doctrine! (Galatians 2. 16.) But as long as a man conceives of himself—as some do —as absolute owner of anything, he may well suppose that he has something to give God as a covering for his sins and as a bid for divine favor.

Only they who profoundly believe that "the earth

is the Lord's, and the fullness thereof," and that man
is the "guest of God," can sing with real understanding
the great hymns of worship, and appreciate the eternal
notes in the historic ritual of the Church.

"No offering of my own I have,
    Nor works my faith to prove;
I can but give the gifts He gave,
    And plead His love for love."
                                    —*John G. Whittier.*

* * *

A Prayer

"My gracious Lord, I own Thy right
    To every service I can pay,
And call it my supreme delight
    To hear Thy dictates and obey." Amen.

Meditation

"The most incongruous, if not ridiculous, sight in
this practical world is a fine machine standing in its
polished beauty, but lacking just the one thing that
gives it motive power or even permits motion. . . .
The instant and commanding thing to be accomplished in the life of Christian people today—and if I
could have my way, this would be what I would see
achieved in every soul—is the experienced presence of
God as the Holy Spirit. It is Pentecost which the
Church needs at once and forever."—*Frank W. Gun-
saulus.*

Morning Song

Give me a song, dear God, in the morning,
    Give me a song at the break of the day,
Give me a song lest the hours grow weary,
    Give me the lift of a song on the way.

Days are so long and burdens so heavy,
  Tired are the faces I see passing by,
They seem so hungry, dear God, and so helpless,
  O how they need some song from on high!

. . . .

So if I covet one gift in the morning,
  It is the shine of the heavens in my face,
Banishing gloom for the worn and the weary,
  Telling the story of infinite grace.

CHAPTER EIGHT

Divine Safeguards

I

The First Fruits

"And now, behold, I have brought the first of the fruit of the ground, which thou, O Jehovah, hast given me" (Deuteronomy 26. 10, A. R. V.).

WILLIAM H. NELSON, in the introduction to his life of General William Booth, *Blood and Fire,* pictures Cecil Rhodes brooding in the lonely grandeur, on the top of a mighty rock, overlooking one of the vast plains of Africa. At length the great Englishman broke the silence, saying to his companion: "I have built a great empire for my country. But look at William Booth. I only wish I could believe what that man believes."

Pathetic picture! How great is the failure of great men who are too busy to give God the recognition due the Creator of the world! It reminds one of the words of the greatest of all philosophers, "What profit is it for a man to gain the whole world and to forfeit his soul?" (Mark 8. 36, Moffatt.) But the tragedy is constantly going on! What can be done for these people—of all kinds great and small—who are leaving God out? Now every man needs God, and yet every man is in danger of letting the busy world crowd Him out. The tides of materialism are forever threatening to engulf us. This is particularly true of the business man. Former Governor William E. Sweet has summed up

187

this peril in the one striking sentence: "How difficult it is for the businessman to live unselfishly! He must bear the handicap of a life whose main purpose is the accumulation of money."

Of course the "main purpose" of any business ought not to be "the accumulation of money." There is no greater task before Christianity just now than the Christianizing of business so that higher motives will control. Years ago Bacon said, "Business should be conducted to the glory of God and to the welfare of the worker." So it should be, and the Church must never rest until this ideal is accomplished in society. But the place to begin is with the individual. Woe to the man who allows the eternal fact of God's ownership of all things to slip out of his mind and heart! The result is a dwarfed and shriveled soul. So it is constantly necessary—day after day and week after week—to hold in the center of one's life this recognition of the Divine Lordship.

But how can this be done? The answer is to be found in the Word of God. From the beginning to the end of the Scriptures our Creator has made loving but indispensable suggestions by which He has sought to safeguard His people against an undue love of the world and the things of the world.

Throughout the Old and New Testaments the Lord repeatedly warns that the surest way to forever recognize the eternal truth of God's constant care and goodness is to establish some unbreakable habit of holy *acknowledgment*. For instance, Christians could well study the beautiful ritual which the Hebrew farmer repeated as he brought "the first fruits" and worshiped before his Creator. He said, "I profess this day unto Jehovah my God, that I am come unto the land which

Jehovah sware unto our fathers to give us" (Deuteronomy 26. 3, A. R. V.). And when the priest had received the offering, by which the worshiper acknowledged his partnership with God, then the man before the altar went on to repeat,

"A Syrian ready to perish was my father; and he went down into Egypt, and sojourned there, few in number; and he became there a nation, mighty, and populous. And the Egyptians dealt ill with us, . . . and we cried unto Jehovah, the God of our Fathers, and Jehovah heard our voice, . . . and brought us forth out of Egypt with a mighty hand, . . . and with wonders; and he hath brought us unto this place, and hath given us this land.... And now, behold, I have brought the first of the fruit of the ground, which thou, O Jehovah, hast given me" (Deuteronomy 26. 5-10, A. R. V.).

* * *

A Prayer

"O Jehovah, thou art exalted as head above all. Both riches and honor come of thee, and thou rulest over all; and in thy hand . . . it is to make great, and to give strength unto all. . . . But who am I, and what is my people, that we should be able to offer so willingly after this sort? for all things come of thee, and of thine own have we given thee. . . . O Jehovah our God, all this store . . . cometh of thy hand, and is all thine own." Amen. (1 Chronicles 29. 11, 12, 14, 16.

Meditation

"Surely, the truth must be that whatsoever in our daily life is lawful and right for us to engage in, is in itself a part of our obedience to God; a part, that is, of our very religion. And whensoever we hear people complaining of the obstructions and hindrances put by the duties of life in the way of devoting themselves to God, we may be sure they are under some false view or other. They do not look upon their daily work as the task God has sent them to do and as obedience to Him."—*H. E. Manning.*

Reborn

I did not know the sky was blue,
   I could not call the morning bright,
Until I heard a still small voice
   And Lo, the world was filled with light!

I did not hear the morning choirs,
   Nor heed the lark upon the wing,
Until I heard Him call, and then
   The universe began to sing!

Deaf, dumb, and blind I walked His earth,
   I breathed His air, a thankless clod,
Until that blessed summer's night
   When my dead soul found life and God!

II

THE FIRSTLINGS OF THE FLOCK

"And Abel, he also brought of the firstlings of his flock and of the fat thereof" (Genesis 4. 4).

That was a lovely picture in our first study: An ancient farmer hastening from the early harvest as evening comes on, standing before the altar of his God and saying, "Here, then, I bring some of the first produce of the land which thou hast given me, O Eternal" (Deuteronomy 26. 10, Moffatt). It was a clear acknowledgment of God's gift of the land and the rain and the sunshine and the power to make things grow. It was like singing sincerely,

"Holy, holy, holy, Lord God of Hosts,
Heaven and earth are full of Thy glory."

But it was not only the farmer who came acknowledging his partnership with Jehovah; the shepherds came also. Abel was a shepherd and we read that he "brought the firstlings of his flock." This is the earliest instance of worship recorded in the Bible, and it is significant that it was not empty handed!

Farther on in the Hebrew history we find that the bringing of the first fruits of the ground and the firstlings of the flock was in accord with the divine commandment that they should bring "the tithe of thy grain, of thy new wine, and of thine oil, and the firstlings of the herd and of thy flock; that thou mayest learn to fear Jehovah thy God always" (Deuteronomy 14. 23, A. R. V.). And this seems to be a part of God's program to safeguard His people from forgetting the Unseen and the Eternal in the midst of a very materialistic existence. Evidently, God's purpose in asking gifts of His people was not merely to get support for the Church—as necessary as this may be—*but to obtain from the worshiper honest and sincere acknowledgment of the Heavenly Father's lovingkindness.*

I think a study of giving in the Bible will make this evident. We frequently use Saint Paul's exhortation to the Corinthians as the pattern for Christian giving. He said, "Upon the first day of the week let every one of you lay by him in store, as God hath prospered

him" (1 Corinthians 16. 2). In Deuteronomy (16. 16)
Moses gives a similar command, "They shall not appear before Jehovah empty;" and goes on to say,
"Every man shall give as he is able, according to the
blessings of Jehovah thy God which he hath given
thee" (16. 17).

Is it not evident that Saint Paul's command to his
churches was out of the Old Testament? The only
difference seems to be that the New Testament exhorts
Christians to do as a matter of loving loyalty what,
in the old dispensation, was made a matter of law.

We can make a very interesting chart of scriptural
giving, and it will bear out our statement above, and
also show that God's primary purpose in asking gifts
of His people was to secure honest acknowledgment
of loyalty and gratitude to a beneficent Creator. Such
a chart would include the following:

1. The "first fruits" (Deuteronomy 26. 10) and the
"firstlings of thy herds" (Deuteronomy 14. 23).

2. "The tenth"—paid by pagans (Genesis 28. 22).

3. "The tenth"—paid by patriarchs (Genesis 28. 22).

4. "Tithes"—paid by Israel (Leviticus 27. 30; Deuteronomy 14. 22, 28).

5. "As prospered" rule for free-will offerings (Deuteronomy 16. 16 and 1 Corinthians 16. 2).

6. "All"—the poor widow (Mark 12. 44).[1]

Each of these Scripture references is worth careful
study, but behind every one of them is the truth that
God is forever seeking, not the gifts but the giver, yet
seeking the giver through his gifts.

---

[1] For part of this chart I am indebted to Dr. David
McConaughy, in *The Money Test*. Fleming H. Revell Company.

"It is not the deed that we do,
　Though the deed be ever so fair;
But the love that the dear Lord looketh for,
　Hidden with lowly care
In the heart of the deed so fair."

* * *

A Prayer

"Thine, O Jehovah, is the greatness, and the power, and the glory: . . . for all that is in the heavens and the earth is thine; thine is the kingdom. . . . O Jehovah, the God of . . . our fathers, keep this for ever in the imagination of the thoughts of the heart of thy people, and prepare their heart unto thee." Amen. (1 Chronicles 29. 11, 18).

Meditation

"For God provides the good things of the world to serve the needs of nature, by the labors of the plowman, the skill and pains of the artisan, and the dangers and traffic of the merchant: these men are, in their calling, the ministers of the Divine Providence and the stewards of creation, and servants of the great family of God. . . . So that no man can complain that his calling takes him off from religion; his calling itself, and his very worldly employment in honest trades and offices, is a serving of God."—*Jeremy Taylor.*

God's Twilight Hour

Dear twilight hour, when blaze of day is done;
　Dear hour of retrospection and of peace!
The heat, the hurry and the stress are gone,
　And evening comes with fragrant sweet release;
God's twilight hour, when fades the day to night,
And I grow conscious of the inner light.

Blest inner light! More clearly let it shine,
Eternal Christ, from Thy great heart to mine;
More clearly let it shine across the years,
Illuminate my joys, dissolve my tears;
So when at last for me comes close of day,
All shall be light along the unknown way!

III

THE HISTORIC ACKNOWLEDGMENT

"Why call ye me, Lord, Lord, and do not the things that I say?" (Luke 6. 46.)

Is not the modern man as sorely tempted as the ancient farmer who brought his "first fruits," or as the shepherd who came to God's altar with "the firstlings of his herds"? In the midst of our complex modern life do we not all need the safeguards that the ancients had, and more?

"Dear Lord and Father of mankind,
    Forgive our foolish ways!
Reclothe us in our rightful mind;
In purer lives Thy service find,
    In deeper reverence, praise."

In the face of the crass materialism of our day many modern churches have written alongside their articles of religion a stewardship creed like the following:

1. *God is the sovereign owner of all things.*

2. *Man is a steward, and must give an account for all entrusted to him.*

3. *God's sovereign ownership and man's stewardship ought to be acknowledged.*

4. *This acknowledgment requires, as its material expression, the setting apart, as an act of worship, of a separate portion of income.*

We are especially concerned with the last two of these articles. Wherever we can make the word "acknowledgment" a burning flame of holy meaning the result will be a new spiritual glow in the Church of Christ. Let us face this issue frankly. It is more than getting a better financial system, although that is needed in thousands of churches. Moreover, the issue is greater than systematic, or even proportionate giving. The real issue is whether a professing Christian is ready to make an honest acknowledgment of God's ownership, and so safeguard his life for companionship with the Eternal.

What is wrong with the person who says, "Oh, I don't believe in this business of setting apart a portion of my income for God; all that I have is the Lord's"? The danger is that such persons become insincere. They may think themselves honest, but they give evidence of the deceitfulness of the human heart.

Here is an amusing illustration told me some years ago by an eyewitness: It happened in a Bible class in Ohio. Two long-time acquaintances came to a good-natured verbal combat. One of the men, the teacher, emphasized the point that God's ownership and man's stewardship ought to be acknowledged by regularly setting apart at least one tenth of income. The member of the class who interrupted the teacher had the reputation of holding his abundant resources with a strong grip. Perhaps this was the reason for the smile that went over the class as he said, "But, Brother Tom, tithing may be all right for some of you; but suppose a man has laid his all on the altar? How about that?"

"How about that?" replied the teacher, while the smiles broke into laughter. *"Well, if I were the Lord*

*and you were the man, I would take ten per cent cash
and call it square."*

A little different experience, but pointing in the
same direction, came to me some years ago in German-
town, Pennsylvania. I was speaking to a national
gathering of a great missionary society. I tried to picture the joy of making business and life a partnership
with God. I prescribed this as a solution to many
problems between capital and labor. I urged all Christians to subscribe to Jesus' platform, "He that loseth his
life shall save it."

When the appeal was finished a keen young woman
arose to her feet and said to the speaker: "I share your
solicitude that Christian people shall be possessed by
the stewardship passion. I believe it must come before
Christ's Church can possess the world; but I want to
ask you one question. You are acquainted with many
who truly are Christian stewards; how did it come
about? *Is it not true that most of them began by ac-
ceptance of the principle of the tithe?"* And there was
only one answer that I could make. It was, "Yes."

* * *

A Prayer

Eternal God, we pray for those whom Thou hast
entrusted with riches. May they not set their hearts
upon them. Help them to know the joy of good stewardship, of faithfully using Thy gifts for the building
of Thy Kingdom. And while we pray for them have
mercy upon us, for Jesus' sake. Amen.

Meditation

"Probably the greatest event of my life occurred on

January 1, 1877. On that day my wife and I made a written vow that we would devote a definite share of our income for religious and humanitarian work, and that this should be a first charge. Since that date we have often increased the proportion, so that the original percentage is left far behind. The distribution of the Lord's portion has been the greatest joy of my life and a real means of grace. It has kept me in constant touch with the promotion of Christlike work of all kinds, and anything I have been able to do for Christ and humanity (including profit-sharing with my work people for over twenty years) has grown out of the vow made thirty-three years ago."—*William B. Hartley.*

God of the Market Place

I love to walk and talk with God
  Along some quiet woodland way,
    Where blows the gentle morning breeze
    And sunrise gilds the altar trees;
  O joy, when in some woodland way
  I can begin with God the day!

But joy still more to talk with God
  Along the busy market place,
    Within the city's constant din
    Where men need God, release from sin;
  O joy, when in the market place
  I can discern the Lord's own face!

If on some holy mountainside
  I hear Thy voice and glimpse Thy face—
    Through all my years I'll bless the day
    I met Thee on the mountain way!
    But better still, dear Lord, I pray
  That Thou wilt give me grace to be
  In rich companionship with Thee
  Along this busy market place,
  Here let me see Thee face to face!

IV

A GREAT DECISION

"Seek ye first the kingdom of God, . . . and all these things shall be added unto you" (Matthew 6. 33).

Out of the Sermon on the Mount comes this great promise. I know how great it is, for years ago it challenged us and after a great struggle we dared to test it. At least in part.

"Do you preach and practice Christian stewardship!" A young preacher was being catechized in the fine home of perhaps the most outstanding layman in New England at that time.

And it was perfectly apparent that the boy preacher didn't know what the "big layman" was talking about. So John Legg proceeded to explain what the Scripture teaching of stewardship had meant to him. Then he told how *the habit of setting aside, for the work of the Kingdom, the first tenth of his income* had given him a new sense of the stewardship of all his possessions.

I well remember that young preacher's first comeback. "Mr. Legg, how do you think that a young preacher, with a new wife, and with a salary of only three hundred and fifty dollars a year, is going to be able to give the Lord the first tenth of his income?"

Well, there was the usual discussion, and it ended by the layman insisting on two points. First, that the habit of tithing-stewardship had brought a great spiritual blessing to his own life. And, finally, that the question was a personal one between each man and his Lord. How we fought with that question! Sometimes we wished that neither John Legg nor his house had ever come into our vision. It was as bad as that! Weeks later we went to the old home in Vermont. I remember saying to my father, "Dad, do you think I ought to give the Lord a tenth of my income?"

He too had never known about "stewardship and tithing," but, after I had explained to him the idea (with his mind fixed, I suppose, upon his boy's small salary), he said in his brusque way, "You give a tenth of your income! In the first place, you don't get any, do you?" Then, coming down to earth, he ended: "Give a tenth? No, I think you'd be a big fool."

I answered, "Well, Dad, I rather feel that way myself. But how do you figure it out?"

Then he proceeded to ask me if I didn't think that if I had gone into some other business I would be getting "a good deal more."

When I agreed, he pointed out, "Then you are really giving the Lord much more than a tenth—the difference between your present salary and what you would have gotten in some other business."

In later years I was to hear many other preachers cherish the same argument. I replied, "Dad, that sounds good to me." And some devil said, "Amen."

We went back to the little church thinking it was all settled. But John Legg's question would not down. Every time we went into the old Book it came up again; and *it is hard preaching when you are afraid of truth!*

To cut the story short, we thank God for John Legg and for the night, some months later, in that little parsonage in Bryantville, Massachusetts, when, after reading from the Sermon on the Mount (Matthew 6. 30-33), a young preacher and his wife got down on their knees to settle the question of whether they would dare to set apart the first tenth of their income for the Church and Kingdom.

Some high-browed brother will smile and some stingy brother will join in, "Rather a trifling matter—this tithing business!" But it was no trifling matter to that young preacher and his wife. It was more than a consecration of money. We know now that it was one of the great decisions of life.

* * *

A Prayer

O Eternal God, who brought again from the dead our Lord Jesus, the Great Shepherd of the sheep, make us fruitful in all things to do Thy will, working in us that which is acceptable in Thy sight. And Thine be the glory forever and ever. Amen.

Meditation

"In regard to money as well as to time, there is a great advantage in its methodical use. Especially is it wise to dedicate a certain portion of our means to purposes of charity and religion, and this is more easily begun in youth than in after life. The greatest advantage of making a little fund of this kind is that when we are asked to give, the competition is not between self on the one hand and charity on the other, but between the different purposes of religion and charity with one another, among which we ought to make the most careful choice. It is desirable that the fund thus devoted should *not be less than one tenth of our means;* and it tends to bring a blessing on the rest."—*William E. Gladstone.*

The Steward's Prayer

Ah, when I look up at the Cross
Where God's great Steward suffered loss
Of life, and shed His blood for me,
A trifling thing it seems to be,
To pay a tithe, dear Lord, to Thee,
Of time or talent, wealth or store—
Full well I know I owe Thee more;
A million times I owe Thee more!

But that is just the reason why
I lift my heart to God on high
And pledge Thee by this portion small,
My life, my love, my all in all.
This holy token at Thy Cross
I know, as gold, must seem but dross,
But in my heart, Lord, Thou dost see
How it has pledged my *all* to Thee,
That I a steward true may be.

V

FIVE REASONS

"Yet for love's sake I rather beseech thee" (Philemon, verse 9).

One of the finest love letters in the world is that which the apostle Paul wrote to his friend Philemon. The story is well known. He is pleading for a former slave, belonging to his friend. Onesimus had run away to Rome. Converted under Paul's ministry, the apostle is now pleading for forgiveness for a changed man. He says, "Although in Christ I would feel quite free to order you to do your duty, I prefer to appeal to you on the ground of love" (Philemon, verse 8, Moffatt). I think this scripture might well describe God's stewardship appeal to Christians.

I have no desire to make any argument that the old law of the tithe is binding on Christians; but why should we not hold ourselves bound by this principle? In the spirit of Paul's appeal I would like to write down some reasons why I believe in the principle of the tithe:

1. *First of all, because I am convinced that the Scriptures teach that every Christian should make an honest acknowledgment of God's ownership and Christ's Lordship over all his material possessions;* this is unescapable for the thinking Christian. It is more than merely obeying the Old Testament law; it is, as Jesus preached, the fulfilling of the law. This is the Christian's pledge of allegiance, and has been, from the beginning, the very heart of the principle of the tithe. We do not make God a mere gift of a fraction of our income, we pay the tithe in order to acknowledge His ownership of all. Professor Harris Franklin Rall gives us this crystal statement: "We do not give to God a fraction of what we possess, but we loyally acknowledge God's sovereignty over the whole. Just now the Church has no bigger need than to have Christian men face this question."

2. *I believe in the tithe principle because I am convinced that to deal honestly with God this acknowledgment must be made regularly as an act of worship.* This for me is as vital as to pray regularly. To fail in this leads to the breaking of the commandment, "Thou shalt not covet," and to the worship of mammon. Systematic giving, as taught in both Old and New Testaments, springs from the principle of the tithe. When Paul said, "Upon the first day of the week let every one of you lay by him in store," he was standing squarely on this ancient principle. And it was not merely to give material support to God's kingdom; it was to cultivate the worshipful heart and mind that

"the first fruits" were demanded. And this is necessary in every age. We must learn to make giving a
matter of worship.

3. *I believe in the principle of the tithe because I am
convinced by Biblical history that an honest acknowledgment of God's ownership of my possessions requires
some definite proportion of my income.* If the tenth is
not that proportion because it comes of the Old Testament, then all systematic giving is to be avoided for the
same reason. "Every man shall give as he is able, according to the blessing of the Lord thy God," comes
from the Old Testament.

No haphazard giving has ever been considered
worthy of an honest worshiper. Moreover, we ought
to be impressed by the historic fact that the practice
of the tithe was not confined to the Hebrew nation,
but was practically universal among the early people.
Doctor Landsell says: "It seems clear, then, in the
light of revelation, and from the practice of, perhaps,
all ancient nations, that the man who denies God's
claim to a portion of the wealth that comes into his
hands, is much akin to a spiritual anarchist. Indeed,
if in the days of Malachi not to pay tithe was accounted robbery, can a Christian who withholds the
tenth be—now, more than then—accounted honest
toward God?"[1]

4. *I believe in paying tithes because I believe in holy
habits as taught in Scripture, and especially in the life
of Jesus.* I believe habits make or break us. Indeed, so
sure am I that a happy Christian life depends upon
some four or five habits, that if some person should
come to me and say, "What must I do to have glad

---

[1] *The Sacred Tenth*, by Dr. Henry Landsell, Vol. I, p. 180.

fellowship with Jesus Christ here and hereafter?" I would prescribe some four or five holy habits, and among them I would say: "Form the holy habit of setting apart a definite proportion of your money for the work of the Kingdom. Make it the first draft upon your income; set it aside with prayer; use it carefully as unto God. Have faith to begin with "at least the tenth." This habit will be for you a trusty thermometer, marking the temper of your spiritual life.

5. *I believe in the principle of the tithe for Christians because a man ought to do as much under the gospel as the Hebrews did under the law;* else, "the motives of the gospel must be inferior to those of Judaism and paganism." In the New Testament the Christian is exhorted to "abound in this grace [of giving] also" (2 Corinthians 8. 7). Can anyone explain how one can "abound" in the grace of giving, and yet give to God a proportion less than the Old Testament required? Dr. J. Campbell White used to say, "The strongest passage in the Bible on the enforcement of the tithe does not say anything directly about tithing. But it states a principle which applies to all the laws of God: 'For the law of the Spirit of life in Christ Jesus made me free from the law of sin and of death. For what the law could not do, in that it was weak through the flesh, God, sending his own Son in the likeness of sinful flesh, and as an offering for sin, condemned sin in the flesh: that the requirement of the law might be fulfilled in us, who walk not after the flesh, but after the spirit.' "

* * *

A Prayer

Most gracious Lord, help us to dare to be gracious

unto Thee. Give us open minds and surrendered
hearts, that we may know Thy truth and so find in
Christ the highest life and joy and peace. Amen.

Meditation

"For what, in dealing with this obligation, did the
Jews not do? They contributed tithes again for the
orphans, widows, and proselytes. Now, however, we
are wont to hear such and such a one say with astonishment, 'So and so gives tithes!' How great a dis-
grace, I ask, is this: that what among the Jews was no
matter of astonishment ... has now among Christians
become a matter of surprise? If it were a dangerous
thing to fail in giving tithes then, to be sure it is much
more dangerous now."—*Chrysostom.*

The Spirit of the Pioneers

Renew their breed, Almighty God,
  Those pioneers of yesterday,
Who through the wilderness and wastes,
  Undaunted pushed their westward way.

Renew their breed, those giant men,
  Those women of the rugged path,
Who smiled at fears and daily gave
  Impossibilities the laugh.

Renew their breed; we need them back
  To scorn the softness of our ways,
We need them back to teach us how
  To meet the problems of these days.

New frontiers lift their rocky heights,
  New deserts stretch before our years,
Renew in us, Almighty God,
  The spirit of the pioneers.

With fortitude they faced their fight
  To tame the unknown and the wild,
They climbed the mountains, plowed the plains,
  To any hardship reconciled.

Renew their breed; we owe them more
 Than we can pay with whines or tears,
Almighty God, renew in us
 The spirit of the pioneers!

VI

SOME MORE REASONS

"Think not that I am come to destroy the law, or the prophets: I am not come to destroy, but to fulfill" (Matthew 5. 17).

Some time ago I received the following paragraph from a district superintendent after he had made the rounds of his churches: "Somebody must get a real heartbreak over this pathetic missionary situation; it haunts me by day and by night. I hear the hard-luck stories in all of our churches, particularly the country and village church, and then I note the fine cars, the bountiful supply of food, good clothes, radios, together with all other evidences of prosperity. And then I wonder just how much ground there is, in reality, for all this complaining of financial stringency. It seems to me it is not a cry for life's necessities, but, rather, a whine for more luxuries." Such a letter adds another answer as to why so many church leaders see the vital importance of the principle of the tithe.

6. *I believe in the principle of the tithe for Christians because experience shows that God's world program is never adequately financed unless His disciples bring their tithes into the storehouse.*

"What would happen," asks Roger Babson, "if every church member in the United States should actually do as the Bible suggests, and set aside one tenth of his income for God? There are about forty million members in our Christian churches, with about forty billion dollars total income. Calculate the tremendous power summed up in one tenth of that amount! Spent wisely such a sum would establish all the additional schools necessary to fit our youth for religious life. It would operate all the hospitals needed to treat all those who must go through life with physical handicaps. It would furnish sufficient money in a few years' time to teach every living soul the principle of righteousness." Certainly, here is food for thought. How can the Church of God become the power in the earth it ought to be until we give to its program a dignified and unfailing support?

7. *I believe in the principle of the tithe just as I believe in the principle of the Sabbath. Wherever it is intelligently followed it has brought spiritual and financial prosperity to individuals and to the Church.* Dr. Robert E. Speer says, "There is no objection that holds against the principle of the tithe that does not hold against the principle of the Sabbath day." Both of these principles rest on the ground of Old Testament sanction and New Testament recognition. Everyone who has conscientiously obeyed either of these principles can testify to the spiritual joy and strength which come with them. Moreover, a careful study of pagan tendencies in our American life of today should convince the open-minded churchman of the imperious need to exalt both of these principles.

8. *I believe in the tithe principle because the decision to pay the tithe has brought spiritual blessing to a great host of people, even marking the beginning of a new religious experience.* "Thirty years ago," says Dr. Charles R. Brown, formerly dean of the Yale Divinity School, "I was induced by a thoughtful layman to inaugurate the habit of giving a tenth. My salary was

only a thousand dollars a year, and to give one tenth of it seemed to make a big hole in it. But when the decision was once made, I was amazed to find how much more I could give and did give than was the case when it was all left to mood and impulse. In all these years I have never seen the day when I was tempted for a moment to return to the old spasmodic, haphazard method of giving to the Lord." This type of testimony can be multiplied ten thousand times.

9. *I believe in the principle of the tithe because for most people the decision to pay the tithe is a challenge to a more heroic faith.* Whether it be true or not that, with most professing Christians, business, pleasure, self come first, and the church takes the last place, it certainly is true that when a man is called to become a tithing-steward he is called to establish, as a life principle, the habit of putting God first. This helps to create a new breed of Christians, who put God and His church where they rightfully belong! It may be possible that in some hour of emotion a man will give out of his possessions or his life, to the point of sacrifice and suffering; but this spasmodic heroism pales before that everyday kind, based on principle and holy habit.

The supreme call to Christian stewardship remains the same. It is the challenge of a patient Christ calling His disciples to a full consecration of life and possessions for the Christian conquest of the world. It is not a renunciation, but a dedication. Christ waits for the churches of this hour to catch the same vision and to make the same heroic dedication that has been made by the heroes of the Cross in every age. We may well keep in mind Bishop Charles Gore's statement, "In the beginning Christianity was kept at a high level by its being dangerous to be a Christian." Why not now?

A Prayer

O Lord Jesus, help us to understand how blessed is the man who endureth prosperity; whose possessions neither turn his head nor his heart; who blesses the world with his substance and joins with God in building the Kingdom on earth. Dear Christ, help me to be this kind of man this day. Amen.

Meditation

"We need some practical abiding principle like this to make sure that the principle of stewardship is a reality in our lives, and that we do not inwardly find ourselves swept into self-deception. It is the easiest thing in the world for a man who does not deal with God in the matter of obligation as he does with his fellows, to find that he has not been giving God his due."—*Dr. Robert E. Speer.*

"Human nature cannot be trusted to carry out its generous impulses. If I should succeed in winding any of you up to the determination to do generous things, you would run down again before next Sunday. That is what a solemn pledge to pay money to God amounts to—a ratchet to hold us up to the pitch we have reached."—*Dr. S. D. Gordon.*

The Presence

There is a peace that passeth understanding;
   There is a joy the world can never know;
There is a light—you will not find it burning
   On any land or sea where'er you go.

This joy of mine is not of earthly making,
   Though you may find it in the sunset's blush;
Above the noise and din of human striving
   There is a Presence and a holy hush!

Peace, precious peace, that passeth human knowledge,
  Peace only such as Christ our Lord can give,
To our surrendered hearts come in thy fullness,
  O come with life that we may truly live!

Sweet peace from Christ, dear witness of His Presence,
  His promised Presence to the world unknown;
In stillness wait we for thy benediction,
  For Thee, dear Christ, we wait, for Thee alone.

VII

A Man Must Live

"I am come that they might have life" (John 10. 10).

> " 'A man must live.' We justify
>   Low shift and trick to treason high.
>   But is it so? Pray tell me why
>   Life at such cost you have to buy;
>   In what religion were you told,
>   *'A man must live'?*"[1]

Never did Jesus say, "A man must live." He did say that a man must die sometimes in order to keep his life alive. "For what is a man profited, if he gain the whole world, and lose his own soul? or what shall a man give in exchange for his soul?" (Matthew 16. 26.)

Some years ago in a New England legislature there was a fight. A pernicious measure had been up for passage. One legislator, upon being reproved for deserting the moral element of the state, excused his perfidy by saying: "Well, a man must live. Once in a while you have to think of your own future."

The answer came back like a flash, "Then, thank God, I have no future!" What about the truth here? Is there any question as to which of the men was right?

---

[1] Charlotte Perkins Stetson.

"Imagine for a battle cry
    From soldiers with a sword to hold,
    From soldiers with a flag unrolled,
The coward's whine, this liar's lie,
  'A man must live.' "[1]

Of course the fundamental question here is, What does life mean? How do you find it. What is it for? Am I here merely to get something for myself? Or is life a stewardship with an eternal goal?

In the end history teaches which is the wiser answer. In the great American debate over the slavery question there is such an answer. Those debates stirred the nation. Was Douglas or Lincoln right? Douglas won that particular election, but Abraham Lincoln won the future! Lincoln said: "I am not bound to win, but I am bound to be true; I am not bound to succeed, but I am bound to live up to what light I have. I must stand by anybody that stands right; stand with him while he is right, and part with him when he goes wrong."

But from another point of view there is an eternally important truth in the words, "A man must live." To this end Jesus said, "I am come that they might have life." It is never important that we live out our three score years and ten; it is forever important that we live while we do live. So many die without ever having lived!

The tragic secret of all such failures lies in a man's living for himself. And the secret of finding life and all that goes with it is, strangely enough, the willingness to give life away to others in faithful stewardship. This was Jesus' philosophy of life.

---

[1] *Ibid.*

> I searched for love,
>   I searched in country and in town;
> I wept because I could not find
>   Love anywhere around!
>
> But when I searched to serve
>   My neighbor, sick and sore,
> Lo! there stood Love, the Beautiful,
>   A-knocking at my door!

This is one of the hardest and most difficult lessons that one has to learn. How strange it is that the fulfillment of one's life lies altogether in the surrender of life. This is the equivalent of William James's assertion that "surrender is the key to every spiritual experience."

So while Jesus' philosophy of life may seem at times to be negative, it always leads to the positive and the joyful in the end. He said, "If any man will come after me, let him deny himself and take up his cross." To the superficial all this seems like taking the joy out of life. On the contrary, it is Love seeking the highest and best in the object of His affection.

> "O Love that wilt not let me go,
>   I rest my weary soul in Thee;
> I give Thee back the life I owe,
> That in Thine ocean depths its flow
>   May richer, fuller be."

* * *

A Prayer

And now, dear God of peace, who brought again from the dead the Great Shepherd of the sheep with the blood of an eternal covenant, even our Lord Jesus, make us ready in all things to seek His will, working in us that which is well pleasing in His sight, through Jesus Christ: to whom be the glory for ever and ever. Amen.

Meditation

"Christ is the absolute Lord of all life. His sovereignty is not constitutional or limited or shared. His writ does not cease to run 'east of Suez' or in time of war or in the complexities of modern civilization. His commandment is not merely a pathetic overstatement of principles which are too easily ignored. He is not one among a number of prophets, and we do not look for another. For the Christian Church the revelation of God in Jesus Christ is finally authoritative in every department of life. Whatever authority conflicts with this is a usurpation. In the sphere of practical life this is the fundamental principle."—*From the Report of the Oxford Conference.*

Easter

I am alive forever,
  This is the word He said,
In Him there is no dying,
  In Him there are no dead;
I am alive forever,
  This is His word to me,
Through springtime after springtime
  To live eternally.

I am alive forever!
  O tell it far and near,
No more can winter trouble,
  Or autumn bring its tear;
I am alive forever,
  Let seasons go or stay
For Christ is my Heart-comrade
  For ever and a day.

Forever and forever!
  O fling it to the breeze,
To live with Him forever,
  Creator of the trees;
To paint with Him the sunsets,
  To visit with the stars,
To flash across God's highways
  Beyond all earthly bars.

I know not how the future
  Shall change me or surprise,
But this will be my Heaven
  To look into His eyes;
To hear again His promise
  As He sweetly welcomes me,
"Thou art alive forever,
  Alive eternally!"

AN EXPLANATION

Readers of the author's books, *Dealing Squarely With God, The Message of Stewardship,* and *The Sharing Life,* will note that some paragraphs from the above are used in several chapters of this book. After consultation with the publishers, this was thought wise in view of the fact that all of the editions of these former publications are now exhausted. It should also be stated that a number of the devotional poems herein used have previously appeared in *Spiritual Hilltops* or in *Practicing the Presence.*

ACKNOWLEDGMENT

The Scripture quotations in this volume taken from the American Standard Version of the Bible are used by permission of The International Council of Religious Education.

Those taken from *The Bible: A New Translation,* by James Moffatt, are reprinted by permission of Harper & Brothers.

FIRST LINES OF DEVOTIONAL VERSE